Those
INCREDIBLE WOMEN
of World War II

Those
INCREDIBLE
WOMEN
of World War II

by Karen Zeinert

The Millbrook Press
Brookfield, Connecticut

Cover photograph courtesy of Carl Mydans, Life Magazine
© Time Inc. Flag photograph courtesy of Comstock.

Photographs courtesy of AP/Wide World: pp. 8, 55; UPI/Bettmann:
pp. 14, 82 (both), 88, 92; Smithsonian Institution: pp. 18 (neg.
no. 86-5614), 24 (neg. no. 85-11122), 26 (neg. no. 85-16994),
31 (neg. no. 86-5616); Franklin D. Roosevelt Library: pp. 29,
79; Women's Army Corps Museum, Fort McClellan, Alabama: pp.
34, 40 (both); National Air and Space Museum, Smithsonian
Institution: pp. 38, (neg. no. A29772); 44 (neg. no. A26421),
59 (neg. no. A56396), 80 (neg. no. A36290); National Archives:
pp. 48, 70, 85; Lee Miller, Margaret Bourke-White Collection,
George Arents Research Library, Syracuse University: p. 62;
Margaret Bourke-White, Life Magazine © Time Inc.: pp. 68, 69;
Carl Mydans, Life Magazine © Time Inc.: p. 72; American Red
Cross: pp. 76; Library of Congress: p. 93; UMI: p. 96.

Library of Congress Cataloging-in-Publication Data
Zeinert, Karen.
Those incredible women of World War II / by Karen Zeinert.
p.   cm.
Includes bibliographical references and index.
Summary: Traces women's struggle to join the battle on all
fronts—in the army and navy and in the air, as correspondents,
as doctors and nurses, and on the home front.
ISBN 1-56294-434-7
1. World War, 1939–1945—Women—United States—Juvenile
literature. 2. World War, 1939–1945—Participation, Female—
Juvenile literature. 3. Women—United States—History—20th
century—Juvenile literature. [1. World War, 1939–1945—
Participation, Female. 2. Women—History—20th century.]
I. Title.
D810W7Z37   1994
940.54′1273′082—dc20   94-2579   CIP   AC

Published by The Millbrook Press, Inc.
2 Old New Milford Road, Brookfield, Connecticut 06804

CONTENTS

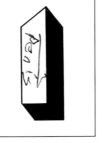

A Chance to Help

Isn't there anything a girl of twenty-three years can
do in the event our country goes to war, except to
sit home and sew and become gray with worrying?

woman's letter to the
New York Herald Tribune

"*These are swell maneuvers for a Sunday morning,*" *remarked a Red Cross observer, when the sky over Pearl Harbor filled with planes. Just moments later the U.S.S. Shaw exploded. The Japanese attack on December 7, 1941, was no maneuver.*

SHORTLY BEFORE eight o'clock in the morning on December 7, 1941, Cornelia Fort, a young flying instructor at an airport located near Honolulu, Hawaii, was giving a college student lessons in taking off and landing. Just as the student began to get ready for his final descent, Fort spotted a military plane heading straight at them. To avoid a collision, she grabbed the controls from her astonished student and pushed the throttle wide open to pull above the oncoming aircraft.

Once Fort reached a safe height, she looked out her window at the scene beneath her. She couldn't believe her eyes when she saw red circles—the national symbol of Japan—on the plane's wings. Then she looked toward Pearl Harbor, an American naval base, and she stared in disbelief at the sight of billowing smoke and sinking ships. Later, recalling the event, she said, "I thought . . . it might be some kind of . . . maneuvers. . . .

"Then I looked way up and saw the formations of silver bombers coming in. I knew the air was not the place for my little baby airplane and I set about landing as quickly as ever I could. A few seconds later a shadow passed over me and simultaneously bullets spattered all around me."[1]

Fort's quick reactions made it possible for her and her student to reach the ground safely that morning. Not all pilots were as fortunate, for the shocking scene Fort had witnessed was an all-out attack on Pearl Harbor, and all ships and planes in the area were potential targets.

Since Japan had not declared war, the attack was a surprise, not only to Fort, but to everyone in the area. In fact, for the first few minutes, some civilians actually watched the beginning of the assault without concern, and they marveled at how realistic defense drills had become.

But when more than 360 Japanese military planes dropped their bombs, and battleships in the harbor erupted in flames, spectators' awe turned to horror.

The bombing of Pearl Harbor was a disaster for the United States. Even though the unsuspecting servicemen put up the best fight they could at a moment's notice, America lost more ships in one hour than it had lost in all of World War I. More than half of the U.S. Navy had been sunk or severely damaged, and 188 aircraft at two nearby bases had been destroyed or damaged. And there were many casualties. More than two thousand men had been killed, and another one thousand had been injured.

———

The United States and Japan had been at odds over Japanese expansion in Asia for many years. Japan's military leaders, who controlled the government, wanted a Pacific empire, and in 1931, they began to build this empire by seizing territory in Manchuria. The United States condemned Japan's actions, but this did little to change the military's behavior. After attacking Manchuria, Japanese troops invaded China, and they established bases in French Indochina, an area now known as Vietnam, Laos, and Cambodia.

The United States believed, correctly, that the Japanese leaders planned to take more territory, including some American possessions. To try to prevent this from happening, the American government stopped all oil shipments from America to Japan in 1940, cutting off 60 percent of its oil supply. Since Japan would have less oil to fuel its battleships and bombers, it would also have less ability to attack other countries—at least that's what the federal government hoped would happen.

But Japan wasn't about to be stopped by a shortage of oil. Japanese leaders simply found new sources. So the American government then tried a different tactic to halt Japanese aggression. In 1941 officials ordered American companies to stop selling any materials to Japan that could be used for military purposes. Officials knew that this would limit the number of ships and weapons that the Japanese could build, and so did the Japanese, since new sources for these items were not readily available.

Japan, realizing that its ambitions were now seriously threatened, tried to negotiate with the United States, hoping to get supplies again. But when Japan refused to give up its dream of an empire, the United States refused to allow trade between the two nations to return to normal.

Almost all of Japan's leaders thought that a major attack would persuade the United States to treat Japan more kindly. Military leaders then decided to take action against America, while pretending to seek peace to keep the United States off guard. Japan actually continued negotiations until it bombed Pearl Harbor. If America failed to heed the lesson and fought back, Japan's leaders believed they had little to fear. Not only did they command a powerful military force, they could count on help from two strong allies, Germany and Italy.

Germany was ruled by Adolf Hitler, the leader of the National Socialist German Workers' Party, or, as it was better known, the Nazi party. Hitler had prepared for war for years, and he commanded a huge army. In the mid-1930s he began to add territory to Germany, first by threats of war, and when that didn't work, by brute force. His army, 1.5 million heavily armed soldiers, invaded Poland on September 1, 1939, and conquered it in four weeks. England and France then declared war on Germany. Hitler responded by launching a massive assault on Great Britain. Then he took Norway, Denmark, Holland, Belgium, Luxembourg, and France in less than three months. In June 1941 the Germans attacked the Soviet Union even though Hitler had promised not to do so. Both the British and the Soviets struggled with all their might to prevent Hitler from conquering them, but the outcome was most uncertain.

Italy was also under the control of a dictator, Benito Mussolini. He wanted an empire in the Mediterranean area and the Middle East. Mussolini began his conquests in 1935 by attacking and occupying

Ethiopia in North Africa. In 1939, Italy took control of Albania, and two years later, it invaded Greece.

Italy, Germany, and Japan had promised to help each other should the United States declare war on any one of them. Known as the Axis Powers, the three nations took great pride in their conquests and their powerful armies, and together they believed they were invincible. Their opponents, which eventually included Great Britain, France, the former Soviet Union, and the United States, were known as the Allied Powers.

When Japanese leaders planned their attack on Pearl Harbor, they doubted that they would need help from other countries, though. They believed America lacked the will to fight. Having watched the United States carefully over the last few years, they noted how reluctant Americans were to become involved in conflicts in either Asia or Europe.

The Japanese were right about America's initial resistance to becoming involved in another war. More than 100,000 Americans had died in World War I, and most Americans wanted above all to avoid more bloodshed. So when fighting broke out in Europe and Asia, the United States tried to remain neutral, refusing to side with any particular country. Congress even passed neutrality acts designed to keep America from supporting one side over another.

America also had a small but strong pacifist movement in the late 1930s. Members were committed to finding peaceful ways to settle disputes between countries, and many thought that all wars were morally wrong. By early 1941 there were about ten thousand pacifists in the United States. They held parades and demonstrations to rally support for their cause, and they pressured American leaders to stay out of the wars in Asia and Europe.

In addition, America had more than 800,000 isolationists, many of whom had real political clout. These men and women insisted that America deal only with problems at home and ignore what was happening abroad. They fought every proposal that had the slightest chance of getting Americans involved in a foreign war, and they backed an amendment to the U.S. Constitution that required a national vote on whether or not America should enter a war, except in the case of attack. The amendment almost passed in Congress.

Although most Americans wanted to remain neutral, as time went on many found it difficult to do so. They were appalled when they learned about Hitler's plan to conquer most of the world and Nazi Germany's horrible treatment of Jews and prisoners of war. There was a general agreement that someone had to stop Hitler, and if European countries couldn't do it, then America would have to enter the war. As a result, the United States ended its neutrality, much to the disgust of the isolationists. America began to send military supplies to Great Britain shortly after it was attacked, and later the United States sent weapons to the Soviets when the Nazis invaded their country. America also sent weapons to China, which the Japanese continued to attack.

Although the United States was becoming more involved in the wars in Europe and Asia, it had stopped short of sending men into battle. This position changed on December 8, when President Franklin Roosevelt asked Congress to declare war on Japan. In his famous speech, Roosevelt said, "Yesterday, December 7, 1941—a date which will live in infamy—the United States of America was suddenly and deliberately attacked by naval and air forces of the Empire of Japan. . . . I ask that the Congress declare that since the unprovoked and dastardly attack by Japan . . . a state of war has existed between the United States and the Japanese Empire."[2] Congress overwhelmingly supported his request.

Shortly after President Roosevelt asked Congress for a declaration of war, Germany and Italy declared war on America. The United States now faced battles on three continents: Africa, Asia, and Europe.

America was not prepared for conflict on such a large scale. Even though there had been a dramatic increase in production in defense plants to supply the Allies, most plants were still far from operating at full capacity. As a result, there weren't enough weapons for a successful war effort. As late as 1940, some American soldiers were drilling with

On the day following the Pearl Harbor attack, President Roosevelt asked Congress to declare war on Japan.

broomsticks instead of guns or threw eggs instead of grenades during drills because there just weren't enough guns and grenades to go around.

In addition to needing weapons, ships, and planes, the U.S. government needed as many pilots, soldiers, sailors, nurses, and doctors as it could muster, as well as tons of medical supplies and food. The United States also had to continue to supply its Allies who could not fight without American weapons and, at the same time, it had to provide basic necessities for citizens on the home front. In short, the demand for manpower was overwhelming.

―――

Yet incredible as it may seem, even though millions of people would be needed for the war effort, at first the federal government was hesitant to turn to American women, 50 million strong, for help in many areas. Like a large part of society, it believed women were limited in what they could do. Nevertheless, some women, such as Cornelia Fort, the pilot at Pearl Harbor, rolled up their sleeves and prepared for war. Few realized how hard some of them would have to fight just for the chance to help their country, and little did their country realize then what extraordinary sacrifices and contributions these incredible women would make in World War II. Just as important, few, if any, Americans foresaw the tremendous changes that were about to take place in society because women demanded the right to help their country win the war, changes that lasted long after victory was declared.

In the Air

☆

We are in a war and we need to fight it with
all our ability and every weapon possible.
Women pilots are a weapon waiting to be used.

Eleanor Roosevelt, First Lady

Delphine Bohn, a flight instructor for the Civilian Pilot Training Program in Amarillo, Texas, poses in a Piper Cub. She would become one of the twenty-seven original members of the WAFS.

ABOUT A YEAR before Pearl Harbor was bombed, Genia Novak, one of the leaders of Women Flyers of America (WFA), stood in front of a room packed with five hundred women in the Plaza Hotel in New York City. "C'mon, gals," she said, challenging her audience. "It's time we got ready to do something for this war that's surely coming. There are a lot of jobs we could do to release men to fight at the front—as mail pilots, pilots of passenger planes, air ambulance pilots. We could fly war planes fresh from the factories to military fields." She paused, then looked around at an audience that was clearly very interested in what she was saying. "Are we going to stay at home and knit mufflers like our mothers?"[1] Apparently few felt like knitting, for many eagerly paid $5 to join the WFA that night, their first step toward becoming a pilot.

The women at the WFA meeting were not alone in their desire to fly, and some of them would join the growing ranks of female pilots in America, a group that included more than three thousand women by the time the United States entered World War II. Women had shown a strong interest in aviation ever since the Wright brothers' first successful flight, and some, like Amelia Earhart, refused to accept the idea that only men could be aviators. These women made their point by taking to the air. Not only did they learn how to fly, they learned how to do it well, setting records in the process. Earhart flew solo across the Atlantic Ocean in 1932 in fourteen hours and fifty-six minutes, an amazing feat then. Ruth Nichols reached new heights, and Phoebe Omelie won cross-country races.

But although many women wanted to fly, few could afford to do so in the early 1930s. Only one fourth of all American women earned their own money at that time, and most of them were poorly paid, receiving, on average, about $850 a year. On-the-ground lessons and flight instruction needed for a license could run anywhere from $500 to $750. So if a woman didn't have wealthy parents or a husband who would pay for lessons, she couldn't become a pilot.

Then, in the late 1930s, some women gained access to a less expensive aviation course, the Civilian Pilot Training Program. This program, financed by the federal government, was developed for young men and women in college. The government said that it had started the program to acquaint young people with flying, the transportation mode of the future, and to help flight schools, which were having a very difficult time financially in the 1930s. These stated goals were given only to avoid alarming the public and agitating the isolationists. The government's actual aim was to develop a large pool of pilots for a conflict that some leaders thought was unavoidable. They were well aware that the current number, about 30,000, would not be enough to win a war.

The Civilian Pilot Training Program was started in 1938. For a $40 registration fee, students received on-the-ground instruction at their colleges and in-the-air training at local airports. Interest was very high, and within one year, more than nine thousand college students had enrolled.

At first, one woman was accepted for every ten men, but in June 1941, suddenly women were no longer allowed to enroll. Those in class could not even finish the course. Needless to say, many women were upset by this decision. One of those most disturbed by it was Eleanor Roosevelt, the president's wife. Mrs. Roosevelt had been a friend of Amelia Earhart, and she was very interested in flying. She wanted to take lessons, but the Secret Service vetoed the idea, deeming it too dangerous. Mrs. Roosevelt was a very active First Lady, and she was not afraid to speak out. When women were excluded from the pilot program, she asked for an explanation.

The Civil Aeronautics Administration, which ran the program, responded quickly. Fearing war at any minute and less afraid than before to announce it, the administration said that the demand for military pilots was now overwhelming, and class space was limited. It no longer made sense to allow women, who could not enter the military, to enroll. Even though many women said they were qualified to fly for the armed services and would do so if given the chance, the government refused to consider the idea, claiming women were too high-strung for the service.

However, although the government was no longer willing to train women, it was willing to hire female pilots to teach men how to fly military aircraft. Even though many women considered this an insult, some female pilots applied to become teachers anyway, for it was a chance to help the war effort. But only a few women were hired, and then only if male instructors couldn't be found.

Women could still take lessons in flying, though, even if the government wouldn't provide them. The Women Flyers of America continued to recruit trainees, and the organization offered inexpensive lessons, $275 for the complete course. Membership rose 900 percent in 1941.

Although many women pilots hoped to use their skills in the military, most doubted that they would be allowed to. So even before the United States went to war, some women went to England, where the British had been fighting the Germans since 1939. These women offered to work for the Air Transport Auxiliary (ATA). This organization of pilots, one fourth of whom were women, ferried planes from manufacturers to the armed services. Although they were well trained, the first American volunteers were not well received.

Pauline Gower joined the ATA in 1940, and she described her first year as very difficult. "We were, quite frankly, unpopular at the start and we had considerable prejudice to break down. . . . We spent the whole of that first winter—and it was one of the most bitter on record—ferrying Tiger Moths all over the country. We could not have had a more severe test. Tiger Moths have open cockpits. . . . None of us will ever forget the pain of thawing out after such flights."[2]

Not only did these pilots deliver planes, they were also responsible for getting nonfighting aircraft off the ground in case of a raid. The pilots took to the skies when their area was attacked and kept their unarmed planes in the air until the bombing stopped. Women proved themselves very capable, and as the need for pilots increased, the ATA began to recruit female pilots in neutral countries.

————

One of the women the ATA turned to for recruiting help was an American, Jacqueline Cochran. Cochran was a well-known pilot who had won five national and international speed records. As early as 1939, she had talked to government officials in the United States about training women to fly for the armed services. Her idea was ignored, but her enthusiasm for such a program never waned. When the British approached her in 1941, she agreed to recruit pilots for them.

To draw attention to the ATA program, Cochran felt she had to do something dramatic. When the United States began to supply its future allies with planes in 1940, pilots working for American companies or the government were forbidden to deliver American-made planes directly to Europe. Instead, the planes were flown to eastern Canada by Americans and ferried to Europe by European pilots. This procedure shortened the distance European pilots had to fly and avoided any possibility of Americans being shot down by German aircraft, which surely would have brought the United States closer to war. To gain media coverage, Cochran decided to ferry a bomber to Great Britain. While this would not seem newsworthy today, flight was so special in the 1940s that passengers who made cross-country flights were honored guests at ladies' luncheons. So the first woman to fly a military plane across the Atlantic would certainly be noticed.

Members of the ATA in Canada did not want Cochran to ferry a bomber. If she failed to reach England, they said, they would be held responsible. On the other hand, if she managed to get to Europe, her success would belittle their jobs. If a woman could do it, flying bombers across the Atlantic would no longer be respected for what it was—a difficult job. The men even threatened to strike if she took a plane to England. To avoid this, a compromise was finally worked out: A male copilot would handle the most difficult situations—the take off and the landing—and Cochran would handle the controls during the rest of the flight.

On June 16, 1941, Cochran and her two-man crew (a navigator also accompanied her) prepared to leave Montreal, Canada, for Prestwick, Scotland. Even though the male pilots had claimed to be satisfied with the compromise worked out between them and Cochran, someone was still angry enough to sabotage her plane. She and her two-man crew had to replace a window that had been smashed in the pilot's cabin. They also had to replace a life raft and a wrench needed to activate the plane's oxygen system, since both had been taken from the bomber. Despite these initial problems, the flight went well, and Cochran received the publicity she wanted. Shortly after, she returned home to find pilots for the ATA. She would eventually send twenty-four women to England.

As soon as she arrived in the United States, she received an invitation to the Roosevelt home at Hyde Park. President and Mrs. Roosevelt wanted to know more about women in the ATA. After a short conference, during which Cochran explained all the things women pilots were doing in England, President Roosevelt asked Cochran to prepare a proposal for using women pilots in the military.

Cochran quickly developed a plan for an organization that would eventually be called the Women's Air Force Service Pilots, or WASP. She envisioned a program that would enable women to ferry all kinds of military planes, a program that would become a permanent part of the armed services.

Meanwhile, General Henry "Hap" Arnold, chief of the Army Air Corps (there wasn't a separate air force then) was having great difficulty finding enough men to ferry planes to military bases. Under pressure from President and Mrs. Roosevelt and impressed with Cochran's well-publicized flight, General Arnold said he was willing to employ women pilots. He contacted Cochran to discuss how this might be done, stressing the fact that even hiring women for the military was controversial, let alone making them part of the armed services. Therefore he didn't believe that it was wise to push for a permanent program. The

Jacqueline Cochran (far left), General "Hap" Arnold (middle), and Nancy Harkness Love (behind Cochran) meet to review a WASP graduation in 1944. These three people were the force behind bringing female pilots into the military.

women, Arnold said, had to prove themselves before that could be discussed.

Although Cochran objected to Arnold's position about not accepting women pilots into the military, she finally agreed to head the WASP. Shortly after, she set up the first training sessions at Howard Hughes Air Field near Houston, Texas. Later the program moved to Avenger Field in Sweetwater. More than 25,000 women inquired about openings in the WASP. Cochran accepted 1,830 applications.

———

While Cochran was organizing her group, another pilot, Nancy Harkness Love, was also preparing women for military flights. Love had learned how to fly when she was sixteen, and she had been ferrying planes to Canada for transfer to France since early 1940. She and her husband operated a very successful aircraft sales company in Boston. Nancy Love's husband was a reserve officer as well as a businessman, and he was recalled as deputy chief of the Air Transport Command shortly before the United States entered the war. As her husband struggled to find ferry pilots, Nancy Love developed a plan for the Women's Auxiliary Ferrying Squadron (WAFS). This plan was accepted by General Arnold, and training sessions were set up near Wilmington, Delaware.

Although the two women's groups had much in common, they had several differences. First, they served different geographic areas. Second, because Love only took women who were already highly skilled pilots, the training programs were not alike. After a short session on army paperwork, Love's pilots were ready to go to work.

Nancy Love, eager to make her program outstanding, set her standards for recruits much higher than those used for male pilots being hired for ferrying. Love's women had to have at least five hundred hours of flight time, for instance, while men were hired after flying for two hundred hours.

Despite her high standards, Love, like Cochran, did not get all she wanted from the military. Her pilots were treated differently from men

Helen Richey (left) and Dorothy Colburn return home to Long Island after ferrying a plane to Canada. Richey would become America's first commercial airline pilot.

who did the same job. Both men and women were hired as civilians for a trial period of ninety days, but only men could become part of the military after that time. Women continued working on ninety-day civilian contracts. Also, men were paid $380 per month while women received $250.

The formation of the WAFS was announced in September 1942. The original group consisted of twenty-seven women handpicked by Love. Among them was Cornelia Fort, the young flying instructor in Hawaii who had witnessed the destruction of Pearl Harbor.

Eventually there was little need for two women's groups whose territories began to overlap. On August 5, 1943, the two merged. From then on, the women were all known as WASPs, and they were headed by Jacqueline Cochran. Nancy Love assisted her.

Flying involved risk, and the WASPs accepted this fact, continuing to ferry even after friends in the program crashed. Thirty-eight women pilots died during the war, and at least one death was caused by sabotage. After several suspicious accidents, Cochran insisted on examining what remained of a plane flown by one of her pilots. She found enough sugar in the gas tank to eventually cause any airplane engine to become clogged and useless. Although Cochran suspected sabotage in other crashes as well, she refused to push for an investigation. She believed that any publicity about this matter would make Americans demand that women be grounded for their own protection, thereby ruining the whole program—the very thing the saboteur wanted to accomplish.

Women pilots made significant contributions to the war effort. More than one thousand flew during the conflict, logging 60 million miles and ferrying more than 75 percent of the planes. They also delivered cargo, tested new aircraft, and towed targets behind their planes so soldiers on the ground could practice shooting at moving objects in the sky—major accomplishments for women who were once regarded as too emotional to fly for the military.

Eleanor Roosevelt

Eleanor Roosevelt served as her husband's personal representative after he was stricken with polio in 1921. She attended political meetings in his place and campaigned for him when he couldn't attend rallies. They made a powerful team. After serving as governor of New York, Franklin D. Roosevelt was elected president of the United States in 1932, 1936, 1940, and 1944.

Eleanor Roosevelt's active life as First Lady was a rarity then. Besides acting as her husband's representative and the official hostess in the White House, she was a mother of six children and author of a column titled "My Day." She used her column to highlight causes that were important to her: a better future for children and equal rights for minorities. She also encouraged the president to appoint women to government posts. In addition, Mrs. Roosevelt worked for many volunteer organizations. During the war, she added visiting wounded soldiers to her busy schedule.

The fact that she chose to be so active in public life surprised her friends, for Eleanor had been a shy young woman who found speaking before crowds an ordeal. But there were so many things she wanted to accomplish, she forced herself to overcome her shyness. She hired a speech coach to improve her speaking skills and deliberately took on challenges to strengthen her self-confidence.

After her husband died, Mrs. Roosevelt continued her career in public service by representing the United States at the newly founded United Nations. She served on the Human Rights Commission in the United Nations for more than seven years, and her leadership abilities earned the respect of many at home and abroad. When she died in 1962, she was hailed as First Lady of the World.

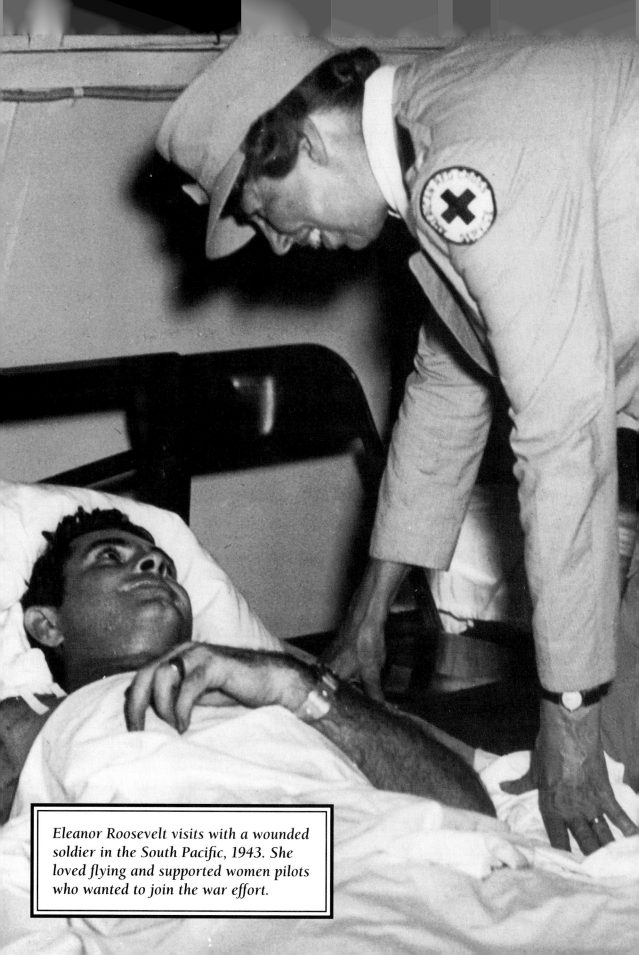

Eleanor Roosevelt visits with a wounded soldier in the South Pacific, 1943. She loved flying and supported women pilots who wanted to join the war effort.

Cornelia Fort

Civilian flying was severely limited after the United States entered World War II, so three months after Pearl Harbor was bombed, Cornelia Fort left her job in Hawaii and returned to her parents' home in Nashville, Tennessee. A few months later, she began to look for some way to help the war effort, and when Nancy Love asked her to join the Women's Auxiliary Ferrying Squadron, she quickly accepted the offer.

By the time Love approached Fort, Cornelia was already a top-notch pilot. She had started flying shortly after she graduated from college in 1939.

After earning her pilot's license, Cornelia worked for the Civilian Pilot Training Program in Colorado. But Cornelia Fort loved speed, and the knowledge that fast planes and good jobs were available at Andrews Flying Service in Hawaii prompted her to leave her teaching position in Colorado and to seek a future with Andrews.

As a member of Love's program, Cornelia was determined to show everyone that women were capable of ferrying every kind of plane available. She took each assignment seriously, for she was afraid that a single mistake would ruin the program.

On March 21, 1943, Fort was flying in formation with six BT-13s over Texas when one of the pilots decided to pull away and do a nosedive to get her attention. His landing gear sliced off part of the left wing of the plane Fort was piloting, and she lost control and crashed.

Cornelia Fort, then twenty-four years old, was the first woman pilot in American history to die while on duty.

Nancy Harkness Love (far left) greets (from left to right) Cornelia Fort, Helen Mary Clark, Teresa James, and Betty Gillies—four of the "Original 27" WAFS recruits. Fort was killed in a plane crash at age twenty-four.

3

On Land and Sea

From long before dawn, recruiting stations
throughout the nation were struggling to keep
pace with the avalanche of patriotic response
unloosed by the call for 540 women candidates
for officers training, all of them motivated by a
common sober impulse—to help with the war.

Josephine Ripley, journalist

Congresswoman Edith Nourse Rogers speaks to the first WAAC officer graduates in 1942, a year and a half after introducing the much debated bill to create the organization.

HE DESIRE of American women to help their country in wartime—even on the battlefield—goes all the way back to the Revolutionary War. One of the most dramatic events occurred in 1776, when the British launched a furious attack on Fort Washington. Advancing redcoats fired volley upon volley of cannon balls and bullets, and outnumbered patriots fell rapidly as they struggled to defend the fort. When colonist Margaret Corbin spotted her husband lying wounded near his gun, she took his place. Margaret loaded his cannon and fired repeatedly at the British before she, too, was wounded.

Corbin was only one of a number of women who accompanied their husbands to the battlefield in the American Revolutionary War. These women, usually no more than six in each unit, cooked and washed clothes for the entire company. In exchange, they were given food from the army's supply depots for themselves and their children. While historians can identify many of the supporting wives by examining supply records, they can't verify how many women served as soldiers. There were some women, such as Deborah Sampson, who wore trousers and shirts and passed themselves off as young men.

The number of women wanting to serve in the military grew over the coming years. Historians have identified women who bore arms, again disguised as men, in the war with Mexico, and they believe that more than four hundred women in trousers fought in the Civil War. During World War I, women offered to help, and the Naval Reserve and the Marine Corps agreed to take some into the armed services when manpower was desperately short at the end of the war. More than 12,000 women volunteered. Most served in traditional roles such as typists. Generals still believed that women were physically and mentally unfit for the sights and sounds of war. Then, in 1940, when a peacetime draft for men was begun, women again asked to join the armed services.

Edith Nourse Rogers, a congressional representative from Massachusetts, introduced legislation to create the Women's Army Auxiliary Corps (WAAC) in May 1941. This bill was simply passed from one committee to another until Army General George Marshall campaigned for the formation of the corps. Marshall needed more office personnel as the army expanded, and he saw no sense in spending a lot of time teaching men to type and file when many women already had these skills. Besides, having a women's corps would mean that more men would be available to fight if America did indeed go to war.

But even though women were willing to enlist and General Marshall wanted to recruit them, some congressmen were strongly opposed to the idea. Representative Hoffman of Michigan, one of the most outspoken opponents, said, "I think it is a . . . reflection upon the . . . manhood of the country to pass a law inviting women to join the armed forces in order to win a battle. Take women into the armed services, who then will do the cooking, the washing, the mending, the humble, homey tasks to which every woman has devoted herself?" Congressman Somers of New York exclaimed, "Think of the humiliation. What has become of the manhood of America?"[1]

Although Hoffman and Somers were determined to defeat the bill, it became a law on May 15, 1942, anyway. The vote in the House of Representatives was 249 to 83. Ninety-six congressmen thought that the proposal was so controversial they wouldn't cast a ballot. There wasn't as much outspoken opposition in the Senate, but that didn't mean that the proposed legislation was well received. More than one third of the senators refused to vote, and the bill passed by a slim margin, 38 to 27. President Roosevelt signed it, and the new law went into effect immediately.

This law made it possible for the army to recruit volunteers for the Women's Army Auxiliary Corps, a separate and temporary unit in the army. By law, volunteers would not have the same rank, pay, or benefits as men who were doing the same jobs in the Army itself, nor could the women expect to remain in the armed services after the war was over.

———

Oveta Culp Hobby was asked to head the WAAC, a position she would hold until 1944 when her health began to fail due to stress and a heavy workload. Hobby had an impressive list of accomplishments by the time she became director of the WAAC in 1942. She was a lawyer (an unusual achievement for a woman then), a successful newspaper and radio executive, and a civic leader. She was also the wife of the former governor of Texas and the mother of two children. After America declared war, Hobby became the head of the Women's Interest Section in the War Department, a bureau that dealt with concerns of mothers and wives of men who had been drafted. As a member of the War Department, Hobby helped General Marshall plan the women's corps. He was so impressed with her ability to lead and make decisions, he asked her to take command when the WAAC became an official organization.

Director Hobby had to create a huge organization from scratch as quickly as possible. One of her first moves was to recruit and train women to serve as officers and instructors. More than 13,000 women applied for 440 positions in the initial officer's training program the first day applications were offered.

The candidates chosen were highly educated, making them part of an elite group. Almost 90 percent had some college education, and 40 percent of the volunteers were college graduates. These women, whose average age was thirty, also had considerable work experience, and they had given up jobs as teachers, editors, social workers, and executive secretaries to serve their country.

The first officer recruits began their six-week training course at Fort Des Moines, Iowa, on July 20, 1942. They studied military customs, leadership, teaching techniques, voice control, court-martial procedures, and army and WAAC organization.

Olveta Culp Hobby was director of the WAAC, the first American military organization of women.

While these volunteers were in training, the Army began to recruit enlisted women, and those chosen, like their officers, also made an elite group. The average age of the volunteers was twenty-four. More than 60 percent were high school graduates at a time when less than 30 percent of enlisted men in the army had a high school diploma. Of this 60 percent, many had some college training. These women passed entrance exams with ease, provided outstanding character references, and like their future officers, survived both a thorough police check on their backgrounds and an extensive physical examination by army doctors.

The first group received four weeks of training at Fort Des Moines, where the women studied a variety of subjects, including military customs. By the end of 1942, another training center had been established at Daytona Beach, Florida. Three months later, training centers opened in Georgia, Massachusetts, and Louisiana.

Hobby hoped to train 12,000 women the first year, and then double the size of the corps to about 25,000 in 1943. But when army generals asked for 80,000 WAACs, Hobby quickly increased the first year's goal to 25,000. Applications came pouring in, and the new organization was swamped with paperwork.

Besides starting a training program, Hobby had to develop a code of conduct for the WAAC. Up to this point, officers had never socialized with enlisted men. It was commonly believed that if officers did so, they would lose their impartiality toward some of the men they commanded. This could cause dissension among the troops and weaken the unit. Hobby had little difficulty with this custom, and she decided that female officers should not become friends with enlisted women.

On the other hand, Hobby had a lot of difficulty deciding whether or not female officers could date enlisted men or if male officers could date enlisted women. When Hobby hesitated to make a ruling, the Army took over. Officers should not socialize with enlisted members of the opposite sex, the generals said. Ever. Still, it was a difficult rule to enforce, and there were many violations.

WAAC officers are sworn into the Army at Fort Des Moines in 1943.

Charity Adams—the first black woman to achieve the rank of major—leads her WAAC platoon. Troops remained segregated during World War II.

Enlisted men and women could date, however, and some fell in love. But since the Army paid no attention to who was dating whom when it assigned and reassigned men and women to bases, most romances were brief and bittersweet.

Pregnancy immediately ended a WAAC's time in the army. If a married woman became pregnant, she was dismissed from the corps, as she would have been in most jobs then. If a single woman became pregnant, which was scandalous in the 1940s, she was given a dishonorable discharge, a step usually reserved for someone who had committed a crime. Any woman who chose to have an abortion also was given a dishonorable discharge, for she had committed a crime. Abortion was illegal in the 1940s except when the life of the mother was threatened.

In addition to deciding what rules WAACs would live by, Hobby also had to decide where WAACs would live. While barracks were available, women were not used to living in buildings that had little or no privacy. Eager to please, the Army then installed some partitions, especially in bathrooms.

In addition, the women's barracks were divided into living quarters for blacks and whites. In the 1940s, much of America was segregated, and blacks and whites attended different schools, played in different parks, and in some towns, even drank from different water fountains. When black women began to enlist, the Army insisted that they live and eat in separate areas, just as black enlisted men did.

Clothing the WAACs proved to be more of a problem than providing comfortable housing. Besides having difficulty deciding what the uniforms should look like, the Army had trouble getting its clothing orders filled. There were no stockpiles from which to draw, and the Army needed thousands of outfits at once. As a result, many of the first volunteers graduated without uniforms. Shortages continued for months, and when winter arrived many enlisted women drilled in the snow in short-sleeved blouses and skirts until jackets and coats could be completed.

Women began to work in many different areas of the military during World War II. These women are air traffic controllers, a job traditionally held by men.

sunk. Although the women survived, their almost fatal experience put the plan to send women overseas on hold.

Shortly after, Director Hobby flew to the training center at Daytona Beach to speak to three hundred women who had been selected to go overseas. Hobby told them how dangerous the positions had become, and she told them that women in the unit were no longer under any obligation to go. Still, she emphasized that WAACs were needed, and she asked for volunteers who were willing to risk their lives.

When Hobby was finished explaining the situation, she dismissed the women for dinner, asking them to think about what they wanted to do while they ate. But, as one of the WAACs in the audience said, "We didn't go to dinner, we all got in line to sign up. The whole battalion, one behind the other. . . . Our dinner was held over for us until we were through. The officers were walking around with tears running down their cheeks, especially [Director] Hobby."[3]

From that point on, WAACs followed the troops. More than eight thousand women served in Africa and Europe, and about five thousand served in Asia. The women were often fewer than 20 miles (32 kilometers) behind the battle lines, and they soon got used to picking up and moving as the soldiers fought their way toward Germany or Japan. They also got used to bombing raids, and more than five hundred women in the Pacific area alone earned combat decorations for their courage and action when the enemy attacked.

Sending women overseas who were not officially part of the Army created a serious problem, for if they were captured, they would not have the protection usually made available to members of the armed services. To remedy this, the WAAC was reorganized on July 2, 1943. Renamed the Women's Army Corps (WAC), the women officially became part of the Army and thus eligible for prisoner-of-war status. WACs also got more benefits and better pay.

Even though the new WAC had more to offer, by 1943 fewer and fewer women were enlisting. There were at least three reasons for the sudden lack of enthusiasm: First of all, the WAC faced serious competition from the other corps. Second, shorthanded manufacturers were now willing to pay women high wages, and many women preferred to help their country in wartime industries where they would not have to give up as much freedom as they might in the military. And third, a slander campaign aimed at the WAC, and indirectly at all the corps and all the 250,000 women who served, made women uneasy about enlisting.

This campaign was so vicious that some Americans thought it was a Nazi plot to ruin the program. Shortly after women had proved they could handle many jobs successfully, rumormongers set out to ruin the women's reputations. Some slanderers claimed that 90 percent of all WACs were prostitutes and that 40 percent of the WACs stationed overseas were pregnant. These stories—and others—spread across army bases, and not all military leaders tried to squelch the lies. Worse yet, some newspapers picked up the rumors and turned them into sensational headlines, spreading the stories even further.

Both the Army and the Federal Bureau of Investigation tried to track down the source of the rumors, but neither had any luck since the stories seemed to spring up everywhere at once. Both felt that "the underlying motive was to degrade military women and drive them out of the 'man's world.' "[4] As one leader of the investigation said, "Men have for centuries used slander against morals as a weapon to keep women out of public life."[5]

Nevertheless, even though WACs were attacked by rumors, they remained dedicated workers, and their outstanding performance earned the praise and respect of many generals. General Dwight D. Eisenhower, who worked with WACs in Africa and Europe, was one of the WAC's best-known supporters. He said, "When this project was proposed . . . like most old soldiers, I was violently against it. . . . Every phase of the record they compiled during the war convinced me of the error of my first reaction. In tasks for which they are particularly suited, WAC's are more valuable than men, and fewer of them are required to perform a given amount of work." And as for behavior, he added, "they were, throughout the war . . . a model for the Army."[6]

4

As Nurses and Doctors

I'm on night duty, twelve hours and it's
really rugged. We're having an air raid again.
I have six wards of patients. Some of them are
frantic. I've given the worst ones all their
ordered sedation. I can hear the Germans go
overhead time after time. You just keep on
doing whatever has to be done. I'm so tired.

June Wandrey, combat nurse

Nurse Jane Kendleigh looks after patients aboard a plane. She was the first Navy flight nurse to serve on a battlefield.

SIXTY AMERICAN NURSES wanted to help the countries fighting against Hitler long before the United States entered World War II. So, like some women pilots who also wanted to help, these women joined forces overseas. The first American nurses to do this began to work for the Red Cross in Great Britain in early 1940.

Most of the nurses had been abroad for almost two years when word of the appalling attack on the United States reached them. They immediately turned to the nearest radio for information. "When the news of the Jap attack at Pearl Harbor came in," said one of the nurses, "we went over to the recreation hall and curled up on the floor to listen to the radio. At two o'clock in the morning we heard the President's speech. Afterward, when the short wave brought us 'The Star Spangled Banner,' we all stood up. We felt so full of emotion we had to gulp and blink our eyes to keep it from spilling out."[1]

These nurses were deeply committed to helping the British war effort, and when America declared war, they were torn between remaining in England and helping their fellow countrymen. After several days of discussing what to do, more than half of the nurses returned to the United States, where their nursing skills would soon be in great demand.

Although women who wanted to serve as pilots or WAACs had to struggle just for a chance to prove they could help the war effort, nurses had no difficulty in finding acceptance. Combat nurses had long ago established the fact that they were up to almost any medical emergency. In fact, their outstanding work in the Spanish-American War in 1898 persuaded Congress to create a permanent Army Nurse Corps (ANC) in 1901. The nurses' skill and courage demonstrated during World War I reinforced their worth, and no one seriously questioned whether or not nurses could work on or near battlefields in World War II.

Even so, there were only seven hundred women in the corps in 1940, and when the Army began to anticipate American involvement in World War II, it also began to recruit nurses. About 43 percent of all civilian nurses volunteered for the ANC, and by April 1941, the Army was taking in almost seven hundred recruits per month. Although the number of volunteers—almost 40,000—was impressive, the Army still wasn't satisfied that it had enough nurses to handle the medical emergencies a full-scale war would entail. Experts predicted that more than 60,000 women would be needed.

So recruiting efforts were stepped up, but no matter how hard the Army tried, it couldn't fill its quota. The Army's failure to do so was partly caused by the serious shortage of nurses at that time. This shortage was so severe, hospital administrators had to shut down whole wings in their buildings in some cities because they didn't have enough nurses to staff them. The future supply of nurses didn't look encouraging either, since many women didn't have enough money to pay nursing school fees.

The Army Nurse Corps also had trouble finding nurses because it couldn't compete with the wages and the free training programs offered by industry. And unlike nursing, which required several years of intensive study, most of the programs for industrial jobs took a few weeks or months to finish. As a result, many potential nurses took jobs in defense plants.

To make matters worse and further limit the number of women available for recruiting, the corps refused to put aside its prejudices. It believed, just as 80 percent of all Americans did then, that married women belonged at home, and the corps refused to accept them as nurses. Also, the corps was very slow to accept black nurses and older women. Since "old" was generally defined as forty-five—thirty at some recruiting stations—many volunteers were turned away. Male nurses weren't encouraged to enlist at any age.

Women who were accepted for the ANC went through a tough four-week training program. Most of the first combat nurses were going to be sent to the deserts in North Africa. Military leaders thought the women should have some exposure to the living conditions they would encounter before they left the United States, so they would be ready to go to work just as soon as they reached their destination. These women trained in deserts in California, where temperatures could soar to 120°F (49°C).

Besides being able to take the heat, combat nurses also had to be prepared to set up hospitals of five hundred beds. To build up physical strength to do this, the nurses hiked 20 miles (32 kilometers) a day, carrying 30-pound (14-kilogram) packs on their backs. They also learned how to treat any available source of water to make it usable, and they practiced keeping drifting sand out of tents so doctors could perform surgery in a reasonably clean environment.

While some nurses would work at evacuation hospitals, caring for the wounded until they could be moved to a more permanent location, mobile nurses' units would provide medical help as soon as possible. They would follow the men as they advanced on the battlefield. These nurses had to be prepared to pull up tent stakes and move every two or three days.

In addition, they had to be prepared to dodge bullets when they were near or in combat zones. To help them survive, the nurses trained on an obstacle course. The course, 75 yards (68 meters) long, contained trenches and barbed wire that the women had to get around while crawling on their stomachs. To give the exercise a touch of reality, instructors threw sticks of dynamite near the trenches and fired rounds of live ammunition just above the nurses' heads. The women learned to get around the obstacles rather quickly, setting records as they hustled along. One nurse crossed 75 yards in seven minutes.

While new volunteers were learning how to survive in the deserts of North Africa, veteran army nurses were already helping wounded servicemen in another hot environment, the South Pacific. Military forces stationed there were no more prepared for attacks than sailors had been at Pearl Harbor. As a result, they had a difficult time defending several U.S. territories, especially the Philippines, where many Americans lived. After receiving heavy shelling in Manila, the capital of the Philippines, American troops abandoned the city and went to the Bataan Peninsula to make a stand. The nurses followed them and set up a hospital in the hot, steamy jungle, which had snakes, rats, and more insects than anyone could count. American forces on Bataan were outnumbered and out-gunned, and they could not hold the peninsula. Just before the troops surrendered, leaders decided to evacuate the nurses. Under the cover of darkness, most were taken in small boats to Corregidor, a nearby island of solid rock, which was under American control at the moment.

Corregidor was also under attack, and these nurses went to work in a hospital that had been established in underground tunnels. The noise from Japanese bombs bursting above them, as well as the sounds of Americans firing back, echoed throughout the tunnels and wore on frayed nerves day after day.

By late April 1942, it was clear that Corregidor also had to be surrendered to the Japanese. Although escape was very difficult, plans were made to try to get as many nurses off the island as possible. Several Catalina flying boats managed to reach the island at night, and some women were put aboard. One of the boats was captured by the Japanese before it could reach safety in Australia, as were more than fifty nurses and fifty doctors who did not have the time or means to get off the island.

One of these nurses, Lieutenant Eunice Young, was helping with a difficult operation when the enemy arrived. She was so busy, she didn't realize that she was a prisoner of war until, as she said later, "I heard a scuffling noise and glanced up. In the door stood a Japanese soldier with his bayonet fixed. This was the first Jap I'd seen, and my heart popped into my mouth."[2]

America's initial losses on the battlefield were high. More than nine hundred victims were brought in each day, and eventually some nurses were trying to care for as many as two hundred men. Usually nurses were assigned no more than ten in a hospital in the United States, where patients seldom needed the intensive care that wounded soldiers required. Many nurses insisted on working twenty-four-hour shifts before dropping with exhaustion on the bare ground somewhere near their patients.

Unfortunately, the incredible losses on the battlefield did not subside, even after the United States was fully geared up for the war effort. This was especially true as Americans and their Allies got closer and closer to Germany and Japan. The soldiers faced experienced, well-equipped, and very determined enemies, and it was not easy to take Italy valley by valley or to storm the beaches of Normandy in France. Nor was it easy for servicemen to inch their way to Japan by conquering one island after another in the Pacific, where more than 50 percent of the first men who landed were wounded or killed.

Medical supplies were quickly exhausted, and nurses had to learn to make do with what they had. When bandages ran out, nurses made their own by tearing up clothing and sheets, and whenever possible, they washed out bloody dressings and reused them. When there weren't enough stretchers to carry the wounded, the women learned that a pair of trousers made a fine substitute. And when blood supplies dwindled, the nurses donated their own.

Army nurses faced some of the greatest hardships and dangers of all women directly involved in the war. More than 200 were killed, and more than 1,600 received medals, including the Purple Heart, a medal given to those wounded by the enemy while serving their country.

The Navy also had a nurse corps, which was started in 1907. However, these women did not serve in combat zones until the end of the war. Instead, patients were brought to them on one of twelve hospital ships located nearby. Naval nurses showed medics—all men—how to give emergency aid at the scene of the disaster before bringing the wounded in for long-term care. Hospital ships were clearly marked, and in theory, they were supposed to be free from any threat of enemy attack. However, there were no guarantees of safety, and some naval nurses, like army nurses, were taken prisoner. Most of them were held in the Philippines.

Sometimes doctors and nurses could not provide the emergency care a wounded soldier required. These patients were flown to hospitals in England, Australia, or the United States where life-saving operations could be performed. Flight attendants were recruited to help the soldiers on these evacuations. In the 1940s, airline attendants had to be registered nurses before they could enroll in flight training programs; therefore, they were ready to go to work immediately. More than 37,000 men were evacuated by air during the war.

———

The demand for nurses on land and sea and in the air was overwhelming, and by early 1943, the nursing shortage was critical. Most women who were going to volunteer had already done so, and many who had volunteered were exhausted. To ease the situation, Representative Frances Bolton of Ohio introduced a bill to create a Student Nurse Corps, which eventually became known as the Cadet Nurse Corps. Bolton's bill would allow the government to pay the tuition of women who wanted to become nurses if the women would agree to serve for the duration of the war plus six months in any nursing capacity. It also provided for refresher courses for older nurses, who were now being recruited. The bill was passed and signed into law in May 1943. However, it still didn't produce the number of nurses needed.

Congress then began to think about the unthinkable—drafting nurses. Some congressmen argued that no country had the right to send men into battle without providing proper medical care. If nurses wouldn't volunteer to help the soldiers, they shouted, draft the women!

These Army nurses landed with American troops during the Allied invasion of the northern coast of France at Normandy. They are having a relaxed meal in front of their field hospital on Omaha Beach.

Although the vast majority of Americans favored such a move, other congressmen weren't ready to take such a drastic step. They argued that forcing women to work in dangerous places was morally wrong. While the representatives and senators gave impassioned pleas for their sides, the war came to an end, and no draft was necessary.

Although nurses had no difficulty in finding acceptance in the war effort, women physicians were shunned. People opposed to the idea of accepting women physicians into the armed services argued that soldiers would be embarrassed if they were examined by women. Besides, opponents added, women were too emotional to be able to perform under the pressures that war presented. These arguments ignored the fact that soldiers were already being examined and treated by female nurses, and to date there had been no complaints by the wounded. Also, opponents ignored the fact that women serving as combat nurses were holding up quite well under the pressures of war.

While a few female physicians tired of trying to gain acceptance into the military and went to England to work with the armed forces there, others decided to fight for the right to serve their country. Led by Dr. Emily Barringer, they gathered petitions of support and hired a well-known public relations expert to present their case to the American people. They also testified at congressional hearings, trying to win over Congress. When Congressman John Sparkman of Alabama introduced a bill that would allow women physicians to serve in the military, female physicians campaigned for the proposal.

Congress finally gave in to the growing pressure, especially when fewer and fewer male doctors were available. On April 16, 1943, President Roosevelt signed a bill granting women the right to be doctors in the military. However, when women physicians learned that most were going to be assigned to WAC units rather than helping as equals in medical combat teams, many refused to enlist. As a result, fewer than one hundred female doctors served in the military in World War II—a tremendous loss of knowledge that might have saved many lives.

Dr. Emily Barringer

Upon graduation from Cornell Medical School in 1901, Emily Dunning Barringer immediately applied for an opening for a physician in a New York City hospital. Although she passed the required test with ease—she received the highest grade among all the applicants—she was not hired because she was a woman.

Undaunted, she continued to look for work. She applied for another opening in New York, and once again she was turned down. On her third try, she was awarded a position that included serving on a horse-drawn ambulance. She was the first woman in America to do this.

Dr. Barringer had a distinguished career. She became a member of the College of Surgeons as well as the New York Academy of Medicine. Later, she headed the gynecology department at Brooklyn Hospital.

When World War II began, she became the leader of the American Medical Women's Association committee set up for the sole purpose of getting women physicians accepted into the military. Barringer testified at congressional hearings often during the war. She pointed out that the supply of male doctors available for the draft was dwindling so rapidly that the armed forces were actually taking male obstetricians into the military rather than accepting women who were much more qualified to deal with battlefield wounds and trauma. Because Barringer knew that few babies were being delivered in combat zones, she considered this a terrible misuse of talent, and she said so repeatedly. She considered the Sparkman Bill a major victory for women physicians, and she was present when President Roosevelt signed the bill into law on April 16, 1943.

Prisoner of War

Nurses captured on Corregidor were taken to the Philippines, where they were held for almost three years. After the war, Lieutenant Eunice F. Young recalled some of her experiences as a prisoner.

"We were to be interned with the civilians at the camp set up on the Santo Tomas University grounds. . . . They crowded us into three trucks. Each truck was guarded by a Jap soldier with a gun. Thus we rolled through the streets of Manila, three truckloads of scared and angry army nurses. . . .

"At the university grounds, we were almost mobbed by the American civilians already interned there. Most of them had husbands or sons or sweethearts on Corregidor or Bataan. They were frantic for news of them.

"Except for an unexpected guardian angel, we would have been cut off completely from the world outside. She was Mrs. Hube, a former U.S. Army nurse who had married a wealthy German in Manila. That gave her German citizenship, and she was not interned. . . . Mrs. Hube talked the Jap high command into permitting her to visit us. She brought us extra food, fruits, the little personal things we needed. Better yet, she brought us news. . . .

"Our living quarters consisted of four rooms, each about twenty by thirty [feet]. . . . In each room were seventeen hard, homemade beds. . . . The grounds were beautiful, but they were not intended to accommodate the 4000 internees eventually crowded inside.

"The Japs decided to allow a hospital in the camp, and we were to be the nursing staff. . . . Taking care of civilians wasn't our rightful job. As army nurses, we should have been with our men in the military camps. We fumed about that, but we accepted the new assignment because we had no choice. . . ."[3]

Army nurses who have been released from the prisoner-of-war camp at Santo Tomas in the Philippines greet a truckload of nurses who have just arrived for duty.

5

As War Correspondents

Sometimes I come away from what I am
photographing sick at heart, with the faces of
people in pain etched as sharply in my mind
as on my negatives. But I go back because I
feel it is my place to make such pictures.
Utter truth is essential.

Margaret Bourke-White, photojournalist

Photojournalist Margaret Bourke-White took pictures of the war for Life magazine. She is standing in front of a U.S. bomber whose engine is called Peggy in her honor.

MOST EDITORS in the early 1900s thought that women journalists should write about "feminine" subjects—weddings and recipes and home decorating. Headline-making stories about murder and mayhem, these editors said, should be covered by men, for women were too delicate to deal with gruesome topics.

Many women journalists, either because they genuinely liked the "feminine beat" or pretended to like it in order to keep their jobs, accepted their editors' positions without question. A few, though, challenged the rules. They wanted to interview government officials, not just their wives, and they wanted to cover major events no matter how grisly they might become. These journalists wanted a chance to seek out stories on their own, keep the public informed, and record history in the making. And they used Nellie Bly as a role model. Bly was a well-known journalist who had taken on dangerous assignments, including posing as an insane woman in a horrible mental institution. If Bly could handle such difficult assignments, the women argued, so could they.

When World War I broke out, some of these women, eager to prove themselves, pleaded for permission to cover the war. Although a few notable journalists such as Bly were allowed to serve as correspondents, editors and war department officials refused to let most journalists go at first, giving in only in the closing days of the war when there was little action to report.

Women continued to push for more difficult assignments after World War I ended, and some editors responded by assigning American women to European cities to work as foreign correspondents. Although most still wrote about traditional feminine subjects, a few began to cover political events for both newspapers and magazines. These correspondents were well-educated—several spoke as many as four foreign languages—and they were very talented. The reports they filed earned the respect of the American public.

One of the most influential and colorful reporters in Europe then was Sigrid Schultz. Schultz worked in Berlin, Germany, for the *Chicago Tribune*. She was a popular hostess as well as a writer, and she often held lavish dinner parties to which she invited famous people of the day. In the early 1930s, she even invited well-known Nazis such as Hermann Goering, who would eventually become the leader of Germany's Air Force. While her guests talked about themselves, Schultz, puffing now and then on a pipe, listened carefully, gathering ideas for articles.

After meeting Hitler and watching his party gain support in the mid-1930s, Schultz became deeply alarmed. Here was a man, she told readers, who would stop at nothing to get what he wanted. She scoffed at American diplomats who believed Hitler's statements about wanting peace, and she warned these diplomats that Hitler was preparing for an all-out war.

Another American journalist, Dorothy Thompson, was also stationed in Germany in the early 1930s. Thompson was working for the *New York Evening Post*, and she was the first woman to head a news bureau in Europe. She interviewed Hitler. In her articles, she made no attempt to hide her contempt for him or his hatred for Jews. This enraged the Nazi leader, and he ordered her to leave Germany in 1934.

Shortly after Thompson returned to the United States, she was hired to write a column for the *New York Herald Tribune*. "On the Record" was eventually picked up by more than two hundred papers, making Thompson one of the most widely read writers in America. She warned readers about Hitler's ambitions, and she ridiculed isolationists for what she thought was an unrealistic stand. Sooner or later, she said, Americans would have to fight Hitler, and the sooner they did so, the easier it would be to defeat him. Thompson, along with Schultz, helped prepare the American public for the likelihood of war. Also, Thompson and Schultz proved that women could write about more than cooking and decorating.

When war actually broke out in Europe in 1939, women correspondents in the area witnessed the events. Editors were only too happy to have someone on the scene, and they sought reports from anyone who had a story to file.

———

As the war spread, foreign correspondents were also sought out as announcers for the major radio networks, the Columbia Broadcasting System, the National Broadcasting System, and Mutual Broadcasting. Competition among the networks was fierce, and each tried to outdo the other with the best reports. There was a common perception that only men could deliver the news. Women's voices were said to lack "authority." However, there weren't enough "authoritative" voices in Europe at the moment, so the networks had to hire some women if they were going to cover all the fast-breaking events.

Since some women correspondents had already covered fighting in Europe, other women journalists assumed that they, too, would be able to report from the front. So after the United States entered the war, women asked the War Department for permission to travel with American forces. But even though many asked, few were given permission and then only under special circumstances.

Sonia Tomara was one of the first women to ask to join American forces in Asia. At first her editor was afraid to send her into such danger. But Tomara refused to give up, and after winning over her editor at the *New York Herald Tribune*, she approached the War Department for the necessary credentials. Here she encountered nothing but stiff resistance. Still unwilling to give up, she turned to Helen Rogers Reid, the vice president of the *Tribune* and a very powerful woman, for help. Reid contacted the War Department and quickly persuaded officials to give Tomara the papers and passes she needed.

Tomara left for Asia in August 1942, and she covered the war in China for her paper. By the time she arrived in China, several male reporters had flown on bombing raids and written exciting accounts of their adventures. Tomara wanted to have the same war experiences as her male colleagues, but public relations officers in the army were very hesitant to allow a woman to join a bombing mission. However, Tomara refused to give up, as usual, and eventually she got her wish.

Many years later she recalled her first experience aboard a bomber. "I went to Kweilin. We had a base there for B-25s, which are medium-sized bombers, and I was put on one of them. You crawl on your belly through to the front of the plane. We flew at about twenty-one thousand feet, which is pretty high without oxygen. There was a bombardier with me, and we had one oxygen mask between us. I took a few puffs and passed it on to him, and then he to me! We flew over Hankow, a big Chinese city where a Japanese military base was located. But we didn't meet our B-24s, the bigger American planes that we were supposed to meet. They flew ahead of us and were attacked by the Japanese Zeroes, their fighter planes. One of our B-24s was downed. . . .

"A couple of Zeroes flew up, but they didn't catch us. . . . We dropped our bombs, whether accurately or not, no one knows. From a height of twenty-one thousand feet, you don't see very much!"[1]

Margaret Bourke-White also wanted to cover the war, and she, too, gained permission to do so with the help of a powerful publisher, Henry R. Luce. Bourke-White was a well-known photojournalist in the 1930s. Her work had appeared in *Fortune* and *Life* magazines, both put out by Luce, and she had published several books as well. In the autumn of 1942, Luce struck a deal with the army. Bourke-White would accompany the troops, taking pictures for *Life* as she went along, and in return, the army could use any photos she took for its news releases and historical files.

Margaret Bourke-White packed six cameras and a few clothes for her first assignment in North Africa. She was a passenger in the ship that carried the first WAAC officers overseas in December 1942. When the ship was torpedoed, Bourke-White, like the officers, spent some frantic hours in a lifeboat, waiting to be rescued.

Once safely on land, Bourke-White decided to take to the air. First she accompanied American pilots when they bombed German forces at

El Aouina in North Africa. She was the first woman photojournalist to record such a mission on film. Later, as American troops fought their way through Italy, she took photos from Piper Cubs. Pilots in these small planes watched for enemy fire or movements, and when they spotted either, they gave the enemy's location to American artillery forces on the ground. Many of the photos she took over Italy were published in 1944 in a book titled *They Called It "Purple Heart Valley": A Combat Chronicle of the War in Italy*.

Later, abandoning the air for land, Bourke-White took photos on the ground in Italy and Germany as the Allies advanced through both countries. She repeatedly recorded the bravery of American soldiers as well as the dedication of members of mobile medical units who worked under incredible conditions to save their patients. Her photographs helped to keep support for the war effort strong on the home front.

Some of her most famous photos are those she took of atrocities committed by the Nazis. Bourke-White was with the army at the end of the war when it entered Buchenwald, a German concentration camp where Jews and political prisoners were literally worked to death. She photographed starving prisoners and piles of corpses and skulls of those who had died.

When other women asked to join Tomara and Bourke-White at the front, the War Department argued that a war zone was no place for a lady. But when WACs were sent overseas, the department found it difficult to deny press passes to women.

To protect the newly accredited women journalists, the department restricted the areas to which women had access. Generally, they had to follow far behind the troops, and this limited their coverage. Also, like all correspondents, their work had to be cleared by censors in the War Department. This was a standard procedure during the war, and it kept vital information such as future troop movements from falling into the hands of the enemy, as well as making sure that correspondents were covering the stories to which they had been assigned.

The first women to be assigned to a particular military unit were

Nuremberg, Germany, after the Allied bombing.
Photograph by Margaret Bourke-White.

German citizens witness the horror of
the Buchenwald concentration camp.
Photograph by Margaret Bourke-White.

War correspondents at a U.S. evacuation hospital in France. Ruth Cowan of The Associated Press is on the left, and Sonia Tomara of the New York Herald Tribune *stands next to her.*

Ruth Cowan, who worked for The Associated Press, a news organization that sold copy to many national newspapers, and Inez Robb of the International News Service, which, like The Associated Press, supplied copy to many papers. Both women were assigned to cover the activities of the WAAC in Africa starting in January 1943.

Cowen and Robb encountered open hostility in Africa. The U.S. Army public relations officer in Algiers was furious when he learned that female correspondents were being assigned to North Africa, and he did little to help the reporters. The chief of the Algiers Bureau of The Associated Press didn't want to work with Cowen, and waiters refused to serve the women in the press corps dining room. When Cowen and Robb objected to this treatment, public relations officers complained bitterly to the War Department, calling the women difficult at best. The War Department used these complaints as an excuse to deny, or at least delay, credentials to other women.

Even so, women continued to press for passes, using whatever clout they had to get to the front. For example, Helen Kirkpatrick, a correspondent for the *Chicago Daily News*, had met several French leaders during her five years in Europe. When war broke out, Kirkpatrick asked for, and eventually received, permission to travel with French troops, thereby avoiding the hassle other correspondents were having with the American War Department. She reported on the war in Africa for six months, then traveled up the Italian peninsula with the Allies.

In the 1940s, newspaper editors did not automatically give bylines to articles. Instead, editors included the author's name only if an article was thought to be exceptional. Helen Kirkpatrick received many bylines for her coverage, and as a result, her reputation spread rapidly. She was so respected for her ability that when the Allies planned their invasion of France in 1944, Kirkpatrick was asked to help leaders make preparations for the press coverage of the event. She remained with the French, even

Marguerite Higgins

Marguerite Higgins covered the war in Europe for the *New York Herald Tribune*. She accompanied a group of Germans who lived near the Buchenwald concentration camp when American military leaders made local Germans look at the horrors committed by the Nazis. Her article was full of gruesome details.

After reading such reports and viewing photos of concentration camps, Americans readily supported trials for Nazi leaders. Higgins wrote:

"The German citizens of Weimar, weeping and protesting the horror of the sight, were led today [April 20, 1945] by American military government officials through . . . Buchenwald concentration camp. . . .

"The men and women were marched past heaps of stiff and naked bodies of people who through starvation, beatings, and torture had died in such great numbers that the Gestapo had not had the opportunity to dispose of them before the American conquest of the camp. At the crematorium where some 200 prisoners were disposed of daily, several women fainted at the sight of half-burnt humans still in the oven. . . .

"[Next the Germans] were taken to a separate 'small camp' where about 200 men had been starved and beaten to a point where they lay dying. The men were so . . . weak that most of them could not raise their voices above a whisper. Under the Nazis they lived in unimaginable filth. . . . The odor of . . . vomit and the smell of death . . . lay heavy over the camp. Two of the men died this afternoon, quietly and without a second glance from their desperately ill companions."[3]

Marguerite Higgins

though she had achieved permission to travel with American troops as well, and she was one of the first correspondents to enter Paris when the Nazis were driven out on August 25, 1944.

—————

While Sonia Tomara, Margaret Bourke-White, and Helen Kirkpatrick continued to cover combat, other women correspondents complained loudly and often when they were restricted from doing so. Newspapers were highly competitive, and there was great pressure on writers to get exclusive news. Those who weren't free to cover all aspects of the war would never be able to compete. Why, the women asked, shouldn't every correspondent be given the same rights? Frustrated with what they considered unreasonable regulations, some writers decided it was time to break the rules to get the stories they wanted. One of the most important scoops of the war—some journalists say *the* scoop—was obtained this way.

While the American, French, and English soldiers fought their way toward Germany from two directions, south and west, the Soviet Union's army was driving toward Germany from the east. Allied leaders had agreed to have the armies from the south, west, and east meet near the Elbe River in the middle of Germany. This would enable all the Allies to conquer some German territory and participate in the final fall of the Nazis. On April 11, 1945, the troops from the south and west approached the Elbe. They set up camp a little west of the river and eagerly awaited the Russians. Needless to say, combat correspondents hovered about, waiting for the first sign of the last Ally, for the arrival of the Soviets meant that the war in Europe was finally over.

Ann Stringer, a correspondent for United Press International, a news service similar to The Associated Press, was not among the correspondents at the front. Stringer had broken one too many rules, and she had been told to pack her bags and leave. She was denied access to local censors, which meant that she couldn't file any story from the front, and was ordered back to Paris.

But Stringer had no intention of returning to Paris—then. Instead, she teamed up with Allan Jackson, a photographer, and on April 25, 1945, they hired two Cub pilots to take them up for an overall view of the Elbe River area. When Stringer's pilot picked up a conversation in Russian on his radio, Stringer ordered him to land in a field on the west side of the river. Jackson's pilot followed. Shortly after, they spotted Russians coming toward them. Jackson and Stringer grabbed a small boat at a nearby dock and crossed the river to greet them.

Although there were language barriers, Stringer got her story and Jackson got his pictures. Now the problem was how to file the exclusive.

Suddenly Stringer decided to follow orders and go to Paris. Carrying Jackson's film and her notes, she ordered her pilot to take her to a nearby air base where she hoped to catch a ride on a military plane. She was successful in persuading a pilot to take her to an airfield outside the city. After landing, Stringer thumbed a ride to Paris. She filed her report and Jackson's film with the censors there, who were not under orders to refuse to take her work.

While she rested in the lobby of a nearby hotel and waited for her scoop to appear in print, a fellow journalist spotted her and expressed surprise at her arrival in Paris. "You should have stayed," he said. "The Russians are coming. That would make a great story."[2] Somehow Stringer kept a straight face.

Ann Stringer's article about the arrival of the Russians was the first of its kind to reach America. She had refused to obey the rules so she could record history. In doing so, she had, somehow, managed to put aside personal grief to do her job as she saw fit. Ann and her husband Bill, also a correspondent, had dreamed of covering the war together from beginning to end. Bill was sent overseas first, and he was killed by a sniper's bullet in France shortly before Ann arrived. Her ability to continue to work at such a time was proof both of her professional dedication and her commitment to a dream.

On the Home Front

On the Home Front

Working is a woman's way
in war time.

Office of War Information

Red Cross workers pack food kits to ship to American prisoners of war.

WOMEN ON the home front, in general, faced fewer dangers than did WASPs, WACs, combat nurses, or war correspondents. They were not exempt from hard work, however, and they encountered many challenges in their homes, as volunteers, and in industry as they tried to help their country defeat the enemy. Their contributions were invaluable.

America needed healthy, well-fed people to do the work required to win the war. Preparing meals was left to women, who were expected to do all household tasks with few appliances to make the job easier. For example, when the United States entered the war, half of the women in America washed clothes, sheets, and towels by hand or in hand-cranked washing machines, and more than one third of them cooked on wood stoves. Meal preparation was time-consuming because there were few convenience foods, and almost all housewives had to prepare their meals from scratch.

Once America entered World War II, feeding one's family became more difficult. Gas and tires were rationed, and using a car for grocery shopping, which had to be done often since iceboxes and refrigerators of the day were small, became a luxury, and in some cases an impossibility. Popular foods, meat, sugar, and many canned fruits and vegetables, were also rationed so there would be enough food to send overseas. While there were other foods available, many, like eggplant, were unfamiliar. To encourage women to use these items, government and state agencies set up classes for housewives in nutrition and health, and women were encouraged to take these courses in their "spare time." The courses often included home nursing topics as well, so women could care for family members and neighbors when illness struck and relieve overworked doctors and nurses on the home front.

In addition, all families were encouraged to have "victory gardens" to increase the amount of food during the war, and women were urged to preserve the surplus for future use. By 1944, more than 75 percent of American housewives were canning, an activity that took lots of time. After the war, one woman recalled her hours of work. "I was canning until midnight, night after night, and I frequently said, 'I wish I had Hitler in that pressure cooker!' "[1]

As busy as women were in their households, it soon became obvious that they would have to assume many new responsibilities to help the war effort as millions of men were drafted. One out of every four women chose to help by joining a volunteer organization.

Understandably, Americans feared more attacks, and one of the first steps taken on the home front was to increase security. Radar was not as common at the beginning of the war as it is today, and aircraft spotters scanned the skies then, looking for enemy planes. The Office of Civilian Defense needed more volunteer spotters, especially on the West Coast, and women filled many of these positions. Women also organized brigades to put out fires caused by incendiary bombs should another attack occur, and they learned how to drive ambulances, give first aid, and help civilians find shelter as well. In addition, some women joined the Civil Air Patrol, which scanned the coasts looking for signs of enemy submarines.

Volunteers were concerned with more than safety at home; they also put in many hours to help Americans overseas. For example, more than three million women joined the Red Cross, one of the largest and best-known organizations in the 1940s. Volunteers in this organization manned blood banks, where by the spring of 1942, five thousand pints of blood were collected each week. They also packed 16 million kits containing candy, gum, and tobacco products for soldiers, and rolled more than 2 billion bandages. In addition, some Red Cross volunteers worked as go-betweens for men and women overseas and their families,

Young Volunteers

High school girls were encouraged to volunteer for organizations designed to help the war effort. These included the Junior Red Cross, the Victory Corps, and the Victory Farm Volunteers.

Junior Red Cross groups were established all over the country, and by the end of the war, more than 19 million boys and girls had become members. Young volunteers packed kits for servicemen, raised money for refugee children overseas, and studied first aid. After completing their first-aid course, many girls worked as aides in local hospitals to help desperately overworked nurses.

The Victory Corps had chapters in many high schools. Girls in this corps operated day nurseries so that women with young children could work in war industries. Members also practiced target shooting with rifles and marched and drilled. On occasion, they were reviewed by military personnel. Government officials hoped these girls would become members of the WACs, WAVES, SPARS, or Marines when old enough.

Another organization, the Victory Farm Volunteers, was part of the Women's Land Army, a volunteer organization that harvested crops when farm workers weren't available. Girls made up 50 percent of the volunteers, and they donated many hours of labor in many areas of the country. Some worked on a particular farm harvesting a single crop such as strawberries or beans before moving on to another assignment. Others spent their whole summer vacation on one farm, helping with everything from cutting hay to milking cows. This program was very successful, and the organization expanded each year, hoping to have as many as 600,000 girls by 1944.

Maryland high-school students founded an organization called Victory Core. Its members ran a day care center to give mothers time for war work.

Hostesses at a USO club in Sioux Falls, South Dakota, entertain airmen on leave from active duty.

sending telegrams when a family member died or a serviceperson was needed at home. The Red Cross also had workers near battlefields and bases in Europe and Asia. Their work was supported by funds raised by volunteers on the home front.

To ease soldiers' loneliness when they entered the service and provide some recreational outlets, several major religious groups formed the United Services Organization (USO) in 1941. The USO established centers on military bases and at major transportation centers in the United States where soldiers could find support. The USO relied heavily upon young women to act as hostesses and dance partners. These volunteers were screened carefully, and their behavior and how they dressed had to be above any criticism.

Women also sold war bonds. These bonds could be redeemed after the war for their purchase price plus interest. Celebrities often helped with sales, and one of the most successful saleswomen was Kate Smith, a popular singer. Smith appeared on the Columbia Broadcasting System on September 21, 1943, for the radio company's War Bond Day. She made regular appeals over a period of eighteen hours, selling more than $39 million dollars worth of bonds. Altogether, volunteers, famous and not so famous, raised $100 billion.

———

While volunteer organizations eagerly accepted the millions of women who wanted to work, industrial leaders debated long and hard about hiring more women. American manufacturers were under great pressure to produce large amounts of war matériel, planes, ships, and weapons, as well as anything else that might lead to victory. This overwhelming demand meant that many new workers would have to be hired at the same time the government was drafting 12 million young men, which severely depleted the number of would-be workers.

But employing women in large numbers, especially in the defense plants, was not an easy thing to do. It required an enormous change in attitude on the part of employers and the public in general. Industry had

Women check cartridges that will go inside the guns of bombers. Many of the women who worked on the home front during the war filled temporary positions left open by men who had gone to the front.

These New England women are producing inflatable boats that will be used by flyers forced to land on water.

long been hesitant to hire women because employers assumed that women were not serious, dedicated workers. Instead, they were thought to be interested only in earning a little spending money. Also, employers expected women to leave their jobs once they married, and supervisors saw no sense in hiring and training workers who would quit within a year or two.

And employers had every reason to assume that most women were little more than temporary workers, for in the 1940s, the pressure on a woman to quit her job after she married was great. Americans believed that a wife's place was at home. How, many wondered, including wives, could a woman handle the many tasks of running a household, care for her children properly (few day-care centers existed then), and hold down a job that typically required a forty-eight-hour work week? Most Americans felt so strongly about this issue that more than 50 percent of them thought Congress should pass a law making it illegal for wives to work.

So industrial leaders, not wanting to face a public outcry over hiring women and fearful that women would not make reliable, long-term workers anyway, tried to fill their positions with men. When the number of available males proved inadequate, employers tried to hire away workers from other companies, offering higher wages and bonuses to attract every male they could. However, eventually manufacturers accepted the fact that they had to employ women if their companies were going to be able to fill orders from the government.

Defense plants began the process of hiring women by first seeking single women, especially those who were already working in some capacity, since these women had proved they were capable workers. When this pool dried up, employers turned to married women.

To avoid public outrage, industrial leaders knew that they had to convince Americans that the United States really needed the help of millions of wives to win the war. Leaders also knew that they had to give women confidence in themselves. For years, society had told them that they couldn't build ships, planes, and tanks. Such jobs were for men only. Now, some long-held beliefs had to be changed overnight. Women who had never worked had to be convinced that they could be riveters, welders, and mechanics. This was a real leap of faith for many wives.

To win over the public, manufacturers turned to the War Advertising Council for help. It created a variety of patriotic advertisements that appeared in popular magazines. These ads portrayed women in defense plants as heroines of the home front, dedicated, determined "production soldiers." The ads also pictured husbands and children clearly proud of the contributions wives and mothers could make. Most ads stressed the fact that the jobs were only for "the duration," that is, the length of the war, to make this prospect of employment less threatening.

Industrial leaders turned to the Office of War Information as well for help in getting women into defense plants. This office had a magazine bureau that made sure that articles and short stories promoting working women appeared in many publications. The bureau even offered to provide plots for stories if writers couldn't think of one.

Actually, almost all forms of media were used to encourage women to join the workforce. Popular songs of the day, such as "Rosie the Riveter," idolized working women. Pleas for workers were read over the radio at regular intervals, and newspaper articles highlighted women working in defense plants to encourage others to join them. In some cities where aircraft industries were especially short-handed, "victory visitors" went door to door, giving short speeches to wives to urge them to become production soldiers.

The stories, ads, and visitors were successful. More than six million women joined the workforce for the first time. About half of these women took jobs as typists, sales clerks, waitresses, and maids, replacing women who had left their old jobs to take positions in defense plants. The other three million new employees went directly to work in industry. All struggled to balance their heavy workloads at home and on the job, and many reported being tired most of the time.

This well-known poster of Rosie the Riveter, commissioned by the War Department, encouraged women to work during the labor shortage caused by the war.

Once women reported for work at the defense plants, it was clear there would be problems. Many classes had to be set up to train new workers. In the past, employees received extensive training, but since workers were needed right away, instructors had to develop new methods for building planes, tanks, and ships. Complicated projects were broken down into several tasks, and each task was assigned to a different person, expanding the assembly-line approach wherever possible.

Another major difficulty was racism. Some white women refused to train with, work beside, or share a bathroom with black women. Many employers tried to avoid possible trouble by refusing to hire blacks. But black women weren't about to be ignored. By 1941, more than 38 percent of them already worked, mostly as maids and cooks. These jobs paid poorly. Now blacks had a chance to help win the war and secure better jobs as well—they called it "double victory"—and they weren't going to let such an opportunity slip away. They were encouraged to seek defense jobs by Mary McLeod Bethune, a black educator, who fought racism in the armed services and defense plants. She was a friend of both President Roosevelt and his wife, and Bethune was not afraid to take her grievances directly to the president. Like Bethune, many black women were also willing to make their plight known. When employers refused to hire them, blacks marched in front of all-white plants with picket signs that read, "Negroes want defense jobs."

While such demonstrations changed some employers' minds, most still refused to change their hiring practices. Blacks then decided to stage a massive protest to force change. More than 100,000 men and women prepared to march on Washington, D.C., carrying banners that read, "We loyal American citizens demand the right to work and fight for our country."[2] To avoid this protest, President Roosevelt issued Executive Order 8802, which outlawed discrimination in defense industries. This order made it much more difficult for employers to refuse to hire blacks, or whites to refuse to work with them. If they did so, the company would lose orders for goods from the government.

Another major hurdle in hiring women was their acceptance by unions. Many war industries had contracts with unions that said that all workers had to be members of the organization that represented their industry, the International Association of Machinists or the United Steelworkers of America, for example. Employers, therefore, could not hire workers who would not join the union or workers the union would not accept. Unions did not want to admit women because they were willing to work for less money than men, and women were seen as unwilling to fight for better salaries in the future, a real threat to men who had families to support. The pressure for more war matériel persuaded most unions—but not all—to accept women, although many limited the role they could play.

Once women were on the job, they faced another problem, the negative attitude of male coworkers. Women received lots of praise and attention for the work they were doing while men doing the same job were ignored. Many men resented this favoritism. Worse yet, men believed that women would threaten their income, not only when the time came to bargain for raises in the future, but every day on the assembly line, where workers were paid for each item they produced. As one female machinist noted, this put real pressure on women. "We worked on a competitive system. You had to keep up with the man standing next to you because he made more money if he could increase his production. If you slowed down, they would say, 'We knew these women would be no good.' "[3]

In addition, many men thought that women couldn't do the job properly, and even when women proved they were good workers, some men were still hesitant to accept them. This woman mechanic's experience was not unusual:

" 'You're a pretty good mechanic,' he said finally, and added, 'for a woman.'

" 'Why for a woman?' I asked and wished I hadn't. I knew what was coming. I had heard it a dozen times before.

Welders at Bethlehem Steel Shipyard in Seattle, Washington, chat between shifts.

" 'Well,' he said, and spat a hunk of tobacco on the floor, 'it ain't women's work.' "[4]

Nevertheless, women took over most welding, riveting, and machinists' positions in shipbuilding, aircraft, and weapons manufacturing. Eventually, their hard work won over most male workers, and few women noted long-term problems. In fact, many reported advantages. One machinist enjoyed working with men because they refused to be bossed around. As a result, she said, ". . . there's more freedom. On the assembly line in '36, I had to ask for permission to get up. . . . Here people walked back and forth and talked freely, and most of the men were friendly."[5]

Besides facing difficulties on the job, women also had difficulty finding proper clothing for work. Although most could buy overalls, uniforms, and snoods (heavy nets to keep their hair out of whirling machinery), many could not find work shoes or work gloves in their size. Most also considered such clothes very unfeminine, for few women in the 1940s wore slacks—let alone overalls—or heavy-soled shoes in public.

Although it took women some time to find and then accept the new clothing styles, they understood that they were necessary for their safety. They knew that working in defense plants was dangerous, and they were reminded of that fact many times as men and women were injured or killed at work. More than 210,000 were permanently disabled during the war, and 37,000 workers were killed. Women had about the same number of accidents as men, even though men were given the most dangerous tasks. This may have been the result of improper training or lack of experience.

The major exception to men holding the most dangerous jobs occurred in the munitions industry. This industry employed large numbers of female workers—only females in some cases. Owners felt that women, especially those who did needlework regularly, had the fine motor skills required to wire fuses on bombs and fill small metal casings with gunpowder without getting blown up in the process. Despite extraordinary safety precautions, accidents still happened. The worst occurred in Maryland in May 1943. Fifteen women were killed in a single explosion, and fifty-four were seriously injured.

Employing almost 19 million women in industry was a major change in American society, not only because it was the first time so many took industrial jobs but because it also caused changes in population patterns. Since not all would-be workers lived near defense plants, more than 25 million men and women, out of a population of 130,000,000, moved—most of them permanently—to cities such as Seattle, San Diego, and Detroit where defense plants were located. This caused serious problems in industrial cities, including housing shortages. When apartments couldn't be found, people crowded into tiny rooms with friends or relatives, slept in cars, or moved into trailer parks, which to the horror of local citizens, were expanding rapidly.

As minorities joined the migration, tensions grew, especially between blacks and whites. Some communities posted signs that told blacks to stay out. When blacks continued to move anyway to find work, race riots erupted, and sometimes they turned deadly. In a riot in Detroit in 1943, for instance, thirty-four people were killed.

Women had more difficulty than men finding a place to live. Single women were looked upon with suspicion, since "decent" young women lived with their parents until they married. Married women with children, whether or not they or their husbands were defense plant workers, had trouble finding housing as well. It was assumed that all children were noisy and messy, and landladies, who had potential renters pounding on their doors daily, could be very fussy. In many cases, rooms were for rent to gentlemen only.

But even though women faced many problems when they decided to work in defense plants, most found that they enjoyed their jobs, and they took pride in their accomplishments. One woman in shipbuilding said, "When we finished one of these beautiful ships, it was an inspiring, thrilling thing."[6] Also, the longer they worked in these jobs, the more they began to feel differently about themselves. Those who lacked self-confidence when they went to work looked at their paychecks with awe. They were amazed that they could earn so much money, more than $1 an hour, and their self-esteem grew as a result.

In addition, women who had worked before America declared war usually had earned less than forty-five cents per hour in jobs traditionally held by women. Now these workers wondered if women shouldn't seek more jobs in industry. They saw the potential of a very different future than they had two or three years before, a future that included a job with a good salary.

At the same time that women's attitudes were changing, industry, again with the help of the War Advertising Council, was preparing another series of ads for publication as soon as the end of the war was in sight. Production soldiers were about to be given an old message—a woman's place is in the home.

Frances Perkins

Frances Perkins, with the strong backing of Eleanor Roosevelt, became the first woman in America to hold a Cabinet position when she agreed to become secretary of labor in 1933. But even though she was well trained for the position—holding degrees in sociology and economics and serving as New York State's industrial commissioner—Perkins encountered many problems.

She had some of her greatest difficulties with women's groups who were struggling for equal rights. These groups fought with Perkins over laws that set working conditions for women. For instance, the number of hours a woman could work, as well as which hours she could work—no night shift—were set by law. Equal rights groups feared that employers would not accept women if they couldn't work the same number of hours as men or take any shift available. Since these groups believed the demand for labor during the war could open up many job opportunities for women, they were especially eager to repeal protective laws.

Frances Perkins, on the other hand, believed that employers would use women's desire to help in the war effort as well as their lack of knowledge about the work place to take advantage of them. Perkins pointed out that women earned less money than men for doing the same job, and she believed that more laws, not fewer, were needed to protect women to make sure they were treated fairly. So during the war, Perkins fought for more legislation, including the Wages and Hours Act.

She served as secretary of labor for twelve years, resigning in May 1945.

Francis Perkins

Japanese-American Women

Although the United States needed as many laborers in defense plants as possible, one group of willing workers was denied the opportunity to help. The Japanese attack on Pearl Harbor stirred up old hatreds in America toward Japanese Americans, as well as fears about their loyalty. A loathsome campaign of lies was started in which Japanese Americans were accused of planning to mine ports along the West Coast and poison the vast food supplies they produced. Some newspaper editors even accused Japanese Americans of arming themselves, preparing for battle in California.

Unfortunately, many Americans believed these lies, and they demanded that something be done to protect the home front. The government's answer, on February 19, 1942, was to order the army to round up 112,000 Japanese Americans, about half of them women, and confine them in internment camps (military camps) where they could do no harm.

The Japanese Americans were forced to sell their homes, farms, and businesses for whatever sum they could get as quickly as possible. Since space at the camps was very limited—each family got one room in the barracks—many also sold as much of their personal property as they could.

Only after proving their loyalty, something that is not easy to do, were any internees allowed to leave the camps. Young women could do this by volunteering to join the ANC or the WAC. But many families needed each member during this trying time, and few women felt they could leave. As a result, most Japanese Americans were held for more than three years.

A Japanese-American child is evacuated with his parents to an internment camp in Owens Valley, California. Japanese Americans were viewed with suspicion, and those who tried to work in defense plants were turned away.

7

Afterword

One afternoon just before the war ended,
they laid off 108 of us. You never heard
so many women crying in all your life.

Ada Habermehl, industrial worker

Mother, when will you stay home again?

Some jubilant day mother *will* stay home again, doing the job she likes best—making a home for you and daddy, when he gets back. She knows that all the hydraulic valves, line support clips and blocks and electric anti-icing equipment that ADEL turns out for airplanes are helping bring that day closer.

Meanwhile she's learning the vital importance of precision in equipment made by ADEL. In her post-war home she'll want appliances with the same high degree of precision and she will get them when ADEL converts its famous *Design Simplicity* to products of equal dependability for home and industry.

ADEL

ADEL PRECISION PRODUCTS CORP.
BURBANK, CALIFORNIA, HUNTINGTON, WEST VIRGINIA
SERVICE OFFICES: DETROIT, HAGERSTOWN, SEATTLE

FOR WAR (AND PEACE) BUY BONDS

> *As the end of the war came into sight and the troops began to come home, advertisements such as this one in the* Saturday Evening Post *spread the message that it was time for working mothers to return to their homes.*

ADEL 'ISOdraulic REMOTE CONTROLS
Built for large aircraft, ADEL's 'ISOdraulic Controls answer remote control problems encountered in rail, marine and industrial applications. Precise positive control thru immediate response of 'slave' unit irrespective of vibration, system pressure fluctuations, temperature (—67°F. to +200°F.). Send for booklet.

mum maintenance assured thru Design Simplicity plus service-testing during 7 years involving millions of miles of operation in all parts of the globe.

DEL EQUIPMENT SERVES UNITED NATIONS' AIR FORCES ON EVERY BATT

W

HEN WAR CORRESPONDENT
Ann Stringer saw the Russians near the Elbe River in Germany in late April 1945, the Allies were only a few days away from declaring victory in Europe. The Italians were defeated and Mussolini had been captured and executed. Hitler, realizing defeat was near, decided to commit suicide rather than be captured. But first he ordered his army to destroy whatever was left in Germany to punish the German people for not fighting harder. Hitler died from a gunshot wound on April 30. Seven days later, the German Army surrendered.

The Japanese continued to fight until two atomic bombs—the first ever used—were dropped on Hiroshima (August 6) and Nagasaki (August 9). The incredible destruction from the bombs, the loss of the support of Italy and Germany, and the fact that the Japanese were losing more and more territory no matter how hard they fought forced them to admit defeat. Japan officially surrendered on September 2, 1945.

In the United States, the joy of victory was tempered by the fact that President Roosevelt, who had been in poor health for some time, had not lived to share the moment he worked so hard to achieve. (Roosevelt died on April 12.)

The joy of victory was also tempered among America's Allies as they looked at the results of years of fighting. More than twenty-seven countries had been at war, and many European cities, villages, and farms had been demolished. Disease was rampant, and starvation was all too common. Because there was so much destruction, historians will never know exactly how many people, civilians and soldiers, died or were wounded. However, many believe that at least 50 million people (322,000 of them Americans) died during the war. Some historians believe that another 16 million people had been wounded (700,000

Americans), while others think that the number may be as high as 75 million.

While world leaders struggled with the enormous problems the war had caused, Americans on the home front quickly turned their attention to getting back to normal. This included disbanding military groups and laying off women in industry. A campaign, planned months before, was unleashed to encourage women to willingly accept old roles again. Ads showing children asking their mothers when they would return home were common, as were articles about juvenile delinquency, which experts now blamed on the lack of discipline children received because mothers worked. Also, surveys indicating that less than 7 percent of all American men wanted a wife who could support herself were hailed as proof that women should quit working.

In addition, industrial leaders reminded women that there were over 12 million servicemen returning, and each of them needed a job. If women insisted on remaining in the workplace, they were told to turn over their tools to the men and head for the typewriters. But even though women faced tremendous pressure to quit—and many genuinely wanted to do so—not all were eager to go back to their kitchens or typing pools.

The story was no different in the armed services. How women fared in the military depended upon how much support they could muster, especially in Congress. For example, the number of WASPs was small, and they had few supporters to fight for a bill to make them part of the military. Even though General Arnold praised the pilots, they were let go in late 1944 when the end of the war was in sight and there was significantly less demand for ferrying services.

On the other hand, Representative Edith Rogers, who introduced the bill that created the WAAC, remained a strong supporter of women in the military, and the reorganized WAC was treated differently because of Rogers's backing. Recognizing the outstanding service women had provided during the war, Representative Rogers asked Congress to make women a permanent part of the armed services. She fought hard for this bill, and it finally became law in 1948.

Over the years, as women earned respect for what they could do in the military, their responsibilities increased. Today most branches have about ten women for every one hundred men, and they serve in almost every capacity, as missile gunners, truck drivers, and, in the old WASP tradition, as pilots. They also serve as part of combat support teams, and women have been given the right to fly combat missions. Women may apply for training at any of the military academies, which were opened to them in 1976. They now make up about 10 percent of the enrollment.

Army and navy nursing corps had strong support in Congress from Frances Bolton, who had introduced the Student Nurse Corps Bill. The demand for nursing help was almost as great in 1945 as it was during the war because there were so many wounded men who needed care. Veteran nurses who had risked their lives were not afraid to make demands, and the armed services realized it had to give nurses more power over their working conditions and higher pay, or it would lose them. Representative Bolton fought for women in the medical corps, and she diligently protected the gains they had made in this area, including the right of female physicians to serve and government-sponsored education for nurses and doctors in the military, male and female.

In light of the work female war correspondents did during the war, editors could no longer deny women headline-making stories. As a result, many were given more responsibility. After 1945, there were three times as many female reporters covering political events in Washington, D.C., for example, as there had been before the war. Still, journalists, competing against each other, were not organized like the nurses were, and they did not have a sponsor in Congress. Therefore, gains were made—slowly—on an individual basis. Today, however, women journalists cover all topics, including men's sports.

Women in industry, the largest portion of women who had joined the war effort, suffered the greatest losses. (Only volunteer organizations lost as many workers after the war, and this was expected, since the need for war bond sales and kits for soldiers overseas had dwindled.) At the beginning of World War II, 95 percent of the women in industry planned to work only until the end of the war. But as the years passed and the war progressed, women realized that they liked their jobs, and they changed their minds. Shortly before victory was declared in 1945, for example, more than 85 percent of the women in the automobile industry, which had made vehicles for the armed services, wanted to keep their positions.

But these women were poorly organized, and they had no one to fight for them. Neither labor unions nor their bosses tried to protect them, and they, like the WASPs and journalists, had no champion in the United States Congress. Industry, therefore, was free to lay off as many women as it wished or to move them into the poorest paying jobs. Almost five million women were forced out of work, and so-called blue-collar jobs, the industrial jobs, were once again a man's domain. Although many women tried to find another job in industry, they had to compete with millions of returning servicemen, most of whom had been promised their old positions. More than 500,000 women never found work again.

Many unemployed women took low-paying jobs as sales clerks, waitresses, or maids. If they had the training and skills they sought white-collar jobs (positions in offices). Ironically, white-collar jobs would become the jobs of the future when millions of industrial positions disappeared thirty and forty years later. However, they paid far less than jobs in industry did. Even so, workers faced intense competition here as well, for the federal government, which hired many typists, clerks, and office managers during the war, laid off thousands of workers when victory was declared.

Although immediately afterward women could not hold onto many of the gains they made during the war, women had proved that they were not as limited in ability as society once thought they were. In achieving this, they opened up opportunities in the following years for themselves and their daughters—opportunities even they, in their wildest dreams, could not have imagined.

PERCENTAGE OF MEN TO WOMEN IN THE WORKFORCE

	1940	1945	1947	1993
In white-collar jobs	65/35%	51/49%	61/39%	64/36%
In blue-collar jobs	74/26%	69/31%	76/24%	81/19%
In agriculture	92/8%	78/22%	89/11%	83/17%
Number of women workers	13,000,000	21,240,000	15,400,000	57,050,000*

* Women now make up 45 percent of the work force, compared to 24 percent of all workers in 1940. The largest portion (70 percent of all working women) hold white collar jobs, one of the fastest growing sectors in the U.S. economy. This chart does not include the service industry, the so-called pink collar jobs, in which more than 17 percent of all working women are employed today.

TIMELINE

1931   Japan invades Manchuria as part of its goal to build an empire in the Pacific.

1934   Dorothy Thompson, American journalist in Germany, warns readers about Hitler's ambitions. First journalist to be forced out of Germany by Hitler.

1935   Italy invades Ethiopia to start its empire.

1936   Germany takes over the Rhineland, the first step in its plans for a European empire.

1937   Japan invades China. Germany, Japan, and Italy sign the Axis Treaty, in which they promise to help each other.

1938   Hitler annexes Austria and part of Czechoslovakia. Civilian Pilot Training Program started.

1939   Hitler takes over rest of Czechoslovakia. He invades Poland on September 1. This is the official beginning of World War II. England and France declare war on Germany. Italy invades Albania.

1940   Hitler's troops take Norway, Denmark, the Netherlands, Belgium, Luxembourg, and France. Italy invades Greece and Egypt.

1941   Hitler declares war on the Soviet Union in June. Women are eliminated from Civilian Pilot Training Program, and Jacqueline Cochran flies a bomber across the Atlantic Ocean in June. On July 1, Cochran begins plans for the WASPs. Japan bombs Pearl Harbor in December. The United States enters the war. Japan goes on to invade Thailand, British Malaya, Guam, Hong Kong, the Philippines, and Midway. One of first prisoner-of-war camps is set up by Japanese in the Philippines. American civilians living in the area are imprisoned.

1942 Nazis push deep into Soviet territory and by fall reach Stalingrad. Bataan falls to Japan in April, Corregidor in May. The WAAC officially begins in May. Other branches of the armed services begin to recruit women in July. The WAFS is organized under Nancy Love in September. Industry begins its campaign to get women to take jobs in defense plants by early fall. Allies begin attacks in North Africa in October. First WAAC officers and first women correspondents to be assigned to a unit go to North Africa in December.

1943 U.S. Marines take Guadalcanal from Japan in February. Cornelia Fort dies in March, first woman pilot in uniform to do so. First women doctors are allowed to enter armed services' medical corps in April. Student Nurse Corps Bill offering scholarships to young women willing to serve during the war becomes law in May. This is the first time the government offers women financial help. Allies declare victory in North Africa in May, invade Sicily in July, and force Italy to surrender in September. German troops continue to fight Allies in Italy.

1944 Soviet troops, driving Nazi soldiers back toward Germany, enter Poland in January. Allies invade Normandy on June 6, which is known as D-Day. Paris is liberated in August. Belgium and Luxembourg are freed in September. Allies prepare to take Germany. U.S. forces, after capturing several Japanese bases, begin a successful drive to take the Philippines.

1945 Allies enter Germany in February and begin march to the Elbe River. Victory over Europe, V-E Day, declared on May 7. Intensive air attacks on Japan begin in May. U.S. Marines continue their drive in the Pacific, capturing Iwo Jima and Okinawa by the end of June. Atomic bombs are dropped on Hiroshima and Nagasaki in August. Japan surrenders, signs a formal treaty on September 2.

NOTES

CHAPTER ONE

1. Deborah G. Douglas, *United States Women in Aviation 1940–1985* (Washington, D.C.: Smithsonian Institution Press, 1990), p. 3.
2. Sherna Berger Gluck, *Rosie the Riveter Revisited: Women, the War, and Social Change* (Boston: Twayne Publishers, 1987), p. 3.

CHAPTER TWO

1. Sally Van Wagenen Keil, *Those Wonderful Women in Their Flying Machines* (New York: Four Directions Press, 1990), p. 74.
2. Doris Weatherford, *American Women and World War II* (New York: Facts on File, 1990), p. 42.

CHAPTER THREE

1. Weatherford, p. 30.
2. Major General Jeanne Holm, *Women in the Military: An Unfinished Revolution* (Novato, California: Presidio Press, 1982) p. 26.
3. Helen Rogan, *Mixed Company: Women in the Modern Army* (New York: G.P. Putnam's Sons, 1981), p. 133.
4. Holm, p. 52.
5. Holm, p. 52.
6. Rogan, p. 146.

CHAPTER FOUR

1. Weatherford, p. 9.
2. Lt. Eunice F. Young, "Three Years Outside This World," *Saturday Evening Post* (May 5, 1945), p. 18.
3. Young, pp. 18, 19, and 89.

CHAPTER FIVE

1. Jean E. Collins, *She Was There: Stories of Pioneering Women Journalists* (New York: Julian Messner, 1980), pp. 82–83.
2. Julia Edwards, *Women of the World: The Great Foreign Correspondents* (Boston: Houghton Mifflin Company, 1988), p. 165.
3. Antoinette May, *Witness to War: A Biography of Marguerite Higgins* (New York: Beaufort Books, Inc., 1983), pp. 83, 84.

CHAPTER SIX

1. D'Ann Campbell, *Women at War with America: Private Lives in a Patriotic Era* (Cambridge, Mass.: Harvard University Press, 1984), p. 181.
2. Miriam Frank, Marilyn Ziebarth, and Connie Field, *The Life and Times of Rosie the Riveter* (Emeryville, Calif.: Clarity Educational Productions, 1982), p. 51.
3. Frank, Ziebarth, and Field, p. 23.
4. Weatherford, p. 148.
5. Frank, Ziebarth, and Field, p. 23.
6. Frank, Ziebarth, and Field, p. 23.

BIBLIOGRAPHY

Blacksmith, E. A., editor. *Women in the Military*. New York: H.W. Wilson Company, 1992.

Blum, John Morton. *V Was for Victory: Politics and American Culture During World War II*. New York: Harcourt Brace Jovanovich, 1979.

Callahan, Sean, editor. *The Photographs of Margaret Bourke-White*. New York: New York Graphic Society, 1972.

Campbell, D'Ann. *Women at War with America; Private Lives in a Patriotic Era*. Cambridge, Mass.: Harvard University Press, 1984.

Douglas, Deborah G. *United States Women in Aviation 1940–1985*. Washington, D.C.: Smithsonian Institution Press, 1990.

Edwards, Julia. *Women of the World: The Great Foreign Correspondents*. Boston: Houghton Mifflin Company, 1988.

Frank, Miriam, and Marilyn Ziebarth and Connie Field. *The Life and Times of Rosie the Riveter*. Emeryville, Calif.: Clarity Educational Productions, 1982.

Gilbo, Patrick F. *The American Red Cross: The First Century*. New York: Harper and Row, 1981.

Gluck, Sherna Berger. *Rosie the Riveter Revisited: Women, the War, and Social Change*. Boston: Twayne Publishers, 1987.

Hartmann, Susan M. *American Women in the 1940s: The Home Front and Beyond*. Boston: Twayne Publishers, 1982.

Holm, Major General Jeanne. *Women in the Military: An Unfinished Revolution*. Novato, Calif.: Presidio Press, 1982.

Honey, Maureen. *Creating Rosie the Riveter*. Amherst, Mass.: The University of Massachusetts Press, 1984.

Keil, Sally Van Wagenen. *Those Wonderful Women in Their Flying Machines*. New York: Four Directions Press, 1990.

Mezerik, A. G. "Getting Rid of the Women." *Atlantic Monthly*, June, 1945.

Mills, Kay. *A Place in the News*. New York: Dodd, Mead and Company, 1988.

Morden, Bettie J. *The Women's Army Corps, 1945–1978*. Washington, D.C.: Center of Military History, United States Army, 1990.

O'Neill, Lois Decker, editor. *The Women's Book of World Records and Achievements*. Garden City, N.Y.: Anchor Press/Doubleday, 1979.

Rogan, Helen. *Mixed Company: Women in the Modern Army*. New York: G.P. Putnam's Sons, 1981.

Rosenberg, Rosalind, *Divided Lives: American Women in the Twentieth Century*. New York: Hill and Wang, 1992.

Sadler, Christine. *America's First Ladies*. New York: Macfadden Books, 1963.

Salzberger, C. L. and the Editors of *American Heritage*. *The American Heritage History of World War II*. New York: American Heritage Publishing Company, 1966.

Verges, Marianne. *On Silver Wings, 1942–1944: The Women Airforce Service Pilots of World War II*. New York: Ballantine Books, 1991.

Walsh, Mary Roth. *"Doctors Wanted. No Women Need Apply": Sexual Barriers in the Medical Profession, 1835–1975*. New Haven, Conn.: Yale University Press, 1977.

Weatherford, Doris. *American Women and World War II*. New York: Facts on File, 1990.

Young, Lt. Eunice F. as told to Frank J. Taylor. "Three Years Outside This World." *Saturday Evening Post*, May 5, 1945.

FURTHER READING

There are few books entirely devoted to women in World War II for young readers. However, some biographies of famous women who were involved in the war are available, and at least a chapter or two in these books focus on the life of the subject during the conflict.

Eleanor Roosevelt has had many biographies written about her, but one of the best illustrated is Robin McKown's *Eleanor Roosevelt's World* (New York: Grosset and Dunlap, 1964). Mary McLeod Bethune, a black educator who fought for equal rights, has been the subject of many biographies also, but one of the oldest, Emma Gelders Sterne's *Mary McLeod Bethune* (New York: Alfred A. Knopf, 1957), has the most information about Bethune's struggle to help blacks during the war.

For more information on journalists, read Jean E. Collins's book, *She Was There: Stories of Pioneering Women Journalists* (New York: Julian Messner, 1980). Besides background on Sonia Tomara, Collins's book tells about the events in the lives of several other World War II correspondents. Also, *Photographing the World: Margaret Bourke-White* by Eleanor H. Ayer (New York: Dillon Press, 1992) contains information on the photojournalist during the war as well as a collection of some of Bourke-White's most famous photos.

Another book of photographs, *An Album of World War II Home Fronts* by Don Lawson (New York: Franklin Watts, 1980), shows what life was like at home both in the United States and Europe. Many pictures include women and children, and they give viewers a sense of what it was like to live then.

Two books discuss women in aviation. Both Carole S. Briggs's book, *At the Controls: Women in Aviation* (Minneapolis: Lerner Publications Company, 1991) and *Sky Stars: the History of Women in Aviation* by Ann Hodgman and Rudy Djabbaroff (New York: Atheneum, 1981) include information about some incredible women in World War II.

INDEX